Best Wishes

Alice Nordale Couch

Lola & Bob Clifton

Alaska Potlatch

Seattle Oct 11 1980

MURDER BY MAIL

AND OTHER
POSTAL INVESTIGATIONS

MURDER BY MAIL

AND OTHER
POSTAL INVESTIGATIONS

ROBERT BRUCE
CLIFTON

DORRANCE & COMPANY   •   *Ardmore, Pennsylvania*

Contents

Author's Note

"I DON'T KNOW WHAT kind of law you is, but you is some kind of law!" Those were the words of a house mailbox thief and check forger who answered our knock at his door early one morning.

The remark surprised me, for I had always believed that the success of much of my undercover work was attributed to the fact that I did not look like a law enforcement officer. I am short, nearsighted, and quiet. It would have been easier to understand if I had been mistaken for a pickpocket or shoplifter. In fact, the United States Attorney at Yakima sometimes called me Willie the Dip when I was working on a case in his bailiwick.

For twenty-four years I was a postal inspector in the oldest law enforcement agency in the federal government. The work of the Inspection Service covers a wide variety of about 250 subjects. The service enjoys a ninety-eight percent conviction rate of those it apprehends. The investigative responsibilities include post office burglary and robbery; theft of mail and post office property; embezzlement; destruction of mailboxes; obstruction of mail; various kinds of mail fraud; extortion letters; mailing of bombs, obscenity material, and poisons; and many other offenses dealing with the postal service.

Murder by Mail, which involved ten years of research, is intended to detail the wide variety of dramatic cases of the elite corps of the Postal Service during the fascinating one hundred years that saw the short life of the pony express, the overland stagecoach, the Railway Mail Service, the pioneer airmail bush pilots, and the dogsled mushers.

Even today, with quick and convenient telephone service,

television, radio, and electronic transfer of funds and messages, there is still a live, vital, and documentary substance to the written word that is a part of the commerce and culture of America. Millions of Americans still entrust their most intimate secrets and most valuable possessions to the United States Mail. It is the duty of every postal inspector to keep this trust inviolate.

When our country was forming, its leaders knew a good mail service would be vital if the diverse multilingual people within its borders were ever to survive as a nation. The French of New Orleans, the Spanish of San Diego, the Mexicans of Santa Fe, the British of Cape Cod, the Russians of Sitka, and some 246 Indian tribes would easily fade apart from one another unless some thread of communication stitched them together. The solution was a grand old mail service that did the job.

It would be almost impossible to give adequate credit to all those who assisted me from time to time in gathering information about some of the older cases. In addition to those whose names are mentioned throughout the book in connection with specific cases, appreciation must be extended to Leo P. Wellnitz of Chicago; former Chief Postal Inspector Henry B. Montague (my boss during the last five years of my service, when I was inspector in charge of the five-state northwest Seattle Division); M.P. "Pat" O'Leary, Alan Pentz, and John Mitcham, all editors of newspapers who found space to print a few of the case histories that are now in this book.

Fred Gosnell of Anchorage, Alaska (now of Seattle), had the foresight to salvage the Railway Mail Service copy of the "U.S. Attorney Letter" in the historic Black Bear Case of Iditerod, Alaska, which was invaluable for factual and historic background.

Leonhard Seppala, the famous dogsled racer; Luella Henry, three times a candidate for president of the National Association of Postmasters; Jo Guertin; and a great many others were of inestimable help.

My wife, Lola, has read reams of copy and remained most patient and encouraging throughout. It is to her I dedicate this book, for she, too, was once a part of that great old postal service we knew and loved.

Any expressed or implied criticisms are intended to be constructive, out of reverence for a once proud U.S. Postal Service.

The title "post office inspector" was changed to "postal inspector" while David H. Stephens was chief inspector.

1

The Siskiyou Mountain Train Holdup

THE TRANQUILLITY of the quiet green valley was suddenly broken by the scream of a steam locomotive's whistle.

The thin crystal air of the high Rockies accepted the unfamiliar sound, and the tall hills echoed it back and forth many times as they savored the impulses of the new vibration before it was slowly muted by the soft cushion of the deep pine forest that covered the steep slopes.

The railroad had arrived, coming as it had to many less-beautiful places in the new country. It offered promise to the land. It was called "progress." It opened an easier way to ship lumber, coal, ore, and livestock to market. It would bring the U.S. Mail.

In the preceding centuries these same hills had seen the quiet movements of the Indians as they crossed the Continental Divide along the old Ute Trail in the shadow of James Peak. The Ute would cross east to go down onto the plains to hunt buffalo. The same trail was also shared by the Arapaho and Cheyenne, who traveled west into the mountains to cut the tall lodgepoles for their winter shelters on the plains.

Then came the mountain men to trap the beavers from their ponds in the mountain meadows and valleys. These rugged frontiersmen traveled from Bent's Fort and Fort St. Vrain on the foothill plains not far away. The self-sufficient mountain men rarely had trouble with the Indians, who believed the great land belonged to all, its bounty to be shared and taken when needed. The beavers had their place in the balance of nature. Their job was to build dams to hold back and catch the rushing spring waters to slow the erosion of the Rockies.

Then came more and more whites; they called them "the 59'ers." They poured like ants onto the hillsides and valleys, frantically searching for gold and silver. Their banners had shouted "Pikes Peak or Bust," and many did "bust;" but there were a few who struck it rich, thereby stimulating an unquenchable thirst in others who stayed on and on, searching the Rockies for their bonanza.

During the winter of 1859, lucky ones like John H. Gregory struck gold not too far away, at Blackhawk, down the gulch from Central City. J. D. Scott and his party struck it rich in lower Boulder Canyon. These and other successful 59'ers took 12 million dollars in gold and 4.4 million dollars in silver out of the Colorado hills west of Denver in one year.

The particular event of a railroad coming into the land of the Arapaho and Ute differed little from the coming of the rails to any other developing area across the wide West. That special culture gendered in the growing towns along the rail belts was unique. I was raised in a new railroad town very shortly after the rails were laid, so I was thrown into a closeness with the ethnic mix and vital developing stage in this part of our nation's youth.

It was here I was to grow and experience the enchantments, disappointments, and fulfillments of this phase of pioneer life and to absorb in depth the everyday living brought about by the development of a new land.

The pine shadows of the main range of the high and mighty Rockies was a wonderful place to enjoy a childhood. At our doorstep were sparkling mountain streams where native trout waited to be caught. There were small mountains all around, and the high peaks of the main Continental Divide was within hiking range. The old abandoned mines and rusting stamp mills were ready to be explored.

Then there were the trains—always a fascination for kids. The double-driver Mallet and the faster Consolidation locomotives drew kids like magnets. Sometimes a rotary snowplow would be left on the wye track to be turned or on a sidetract—those monsters never lost their charm.

My boyhood chum of those days was David Ramaley, whose folks spent the summer in a house near ours. David and I were soon hooking rides on the slow freight trains that climbed into the clouds, going west from our elevation of 9,000 feet to 11,660 before they crossed the Continental Divide. A great many switchbacks were needed to make the climb, and a kid could hook a nine-mile ride; jump off the slow, struggling freight; then be home after a short hike of little more than three miles sharply downhill. Occasionally a brakeman would summarily order us to get out of a gondola car and off the train, but that was rare.

At home we played trains with a passion. We built wyes, switch-backs, tunnels, bridges, curves, and sidetracks along the face of the excavation cut for our house or in a sandpile. Our trains were short pieces of lath coupled with string. Some of the older kids built mock trains using packing boxes, and the cylindrical banana crates became the boilers of the locomotives. Every kid was sure he would be a railroad engineer when he grew up. Bill Crane was the only one who actually did become one.

There were always chores to do—filling the kerosene lamps we used for light at night; chopping wood for the heating stove; carrying water from the town well in buckets; and stocking the shelves in my dad's store—always putting the new merchandise behind the old so that none of it would get too shelf worn.

Whenever we meet (which is rarely these days), David Ramaley reminds me of those days, which were free of any real responsibilities of youth, adding to the joys of childhood, when life is somewhere between make-believe and an experiment. Every new thing is a delight—a fresh joy—that only a child can appreciate. There were fortifications waiting to be discovered along the old Indian trails, where arrowheads could be found.

The local deliveries from the store were made by my uncle, driving a wagon drawn by a team of horses. Supplies needed to be taken deep into the nearby hills to supply the miners. It was always important for a boy to go along on these trips. And Uncle Ed Evans *never* could refuse a nephew's plea to go along.

While the railroad was being built, there were construction camps. The one in Boulder Park that sprang up was called Ragtown, a conglomeration of half-frame, half-tent shacks. Any crew of rough construction men work hard, and they play hard, too. There was little diversion from work in Ragtown. The high-stake poker and dice games after each payday were soon in full swing. Naturally, there were women. One of the shacks bore a crudely painted sign that read HORE HOUSE. The going rate for such services was one silver dollar. A few girls, probably fore-runners of today's call girls, packed narrow mattresses about town, giving curb service where needed, so to speak.

About a mile off the rail route was the existing town of Baltimore, where added amusement could be found. Baltimore had a saloon, a poolroom, an opera house, and several log cabins. Since Ragtown was dry, the saloon at Baltimore drew a host of gandy dancers from the construction crews. There was also a post office at Baltimore. Mail came nine miles over the hills from the county seat at Central City, carried by wagon in summer and by a man on snowshoes in winter. John Hatfield ran the saloon and was also postmaster.

Post Office Inspector Fredericks visited Baltimore in the summer of 1904 to make an inspection of the office. Postmaster Hatfield was offered the choice of giving up either the saloon or the post office. Hatfield was making money and having too much fun as bartender, so he decided to give up the post office.

Being the only reasonably level ground in the mountains along the railroad right-of-way west of Denver, Boulder Park was the logical place to build a division point. A depot, water tank, coal chute, roundhouse, wye, dance pavilion, and restaurant were soon built by the railroad. This work was done about a mile from both Ragtown and Baltimore, and the new town was called Tolland.

The name Tolland was selected in honor of Katharine Ellen Toll who had given the railroad a right-of-way through Boulder Park. The Toll family platted a town and built a twenty-room, two-story

4

hotel called the Toll Inn. This establishment, which cost about five thousand dollars at the time, was an elaborate frame structure with battery-operated lights and piped-in water carried through wooden conduits. Mrs. Toll said that Tolland, pronounced to rhyme with Holland, was her ancestral homesite in southeast England. The plat of the town prohibited the sale of liquor.

When the railroad came, the local people turned from the unrewarding search for gold to working for the railroad or finding work created by its arrival. The grade for the new line was formed with horse-drawn fresnos and pig-nosed earth movers. The work was done by men, mules, and horses.

The opportunity for another hotel, restaurant, and grocery in Tolland appealed to my grandmother, who had lived in Baltimore. With the physical help from her son, Lewis, and with financial help from her daughters, she had a building constructed across from the new railroad depot. The post office was moved from Baltimore to Tolland, and my mother was appointed postmaster on September 27, 1904, a position she retained until her death. The post office part of the building was located in the rear of the grocery, a typical location for small-town post offices. Everyone in town who came for mail had to pass by the store shelves, counters, and merchandise displays. Dad ran the grocery store.

With the entire family working in the new store and hotel, I became acquainted with the postal service when I was still crawling around in diapers. When I became a little older, I can remember mother telling me I was not to go into the post office enclosure because it was for government business only. This admonition went pretty well unheeded. I was to be in and out of that post office and a great many more, in one capacity or another, through most of my life.

When the train brought the mail, it would be dumped from the pouch onto the worktable and then sorted. Almost everyone in town would gather in the store to talk with neighbors until the mail was sorted. When the mail was ready, mother would open the tiny swinging window doors in the post office screen line and call out, "All up!"

A line at the window grew immediately. Watching this scene

reenacted everyday made me realize that the arrival of the mail was actually the highlight of the day for many. Nothing can brighten a day as much as a letter from home. If the train was late or arrived at night, it was customary for mother to open the post office whenever the mail did arrive.

In those days before the widespread use of the telephone, telegraph, radio, and other means of communication, mail was a highly important thing. The United States Mail was a sort of miracle—a miracle of dependability, of security, and often of speed. Nothing can be as consistently uplifting as a letter from home, whether it is delivered on the field of war, within the halls of learning, or over the frozen tundra of Alaska.

Response to the arrival of mail always causes a deep-seated reaction whether announced by mother's "All up" or by an overseas army sergeant's "Mail call!"

I learned at an early age what a good mail service meant to the personal and business lives of a community.

As I grew, the town of Tolland grew, just as similar whistle-stops along the routes of other railroads grew. The Union Pacific, the Northern Pacific, the Great Northern, the Santa Fe, and others created the environment that fostered the fast growth of hundreds of small towns. Like many others, Tolland soon had its own newspaper, dance hall, pool hall, shoemaker, school, grocer, and stockyard; but, unlike others, it had neither a saloon nor a bank. There was a typical American cross-section of people from German, Italian, Mexican, Spanish, French, Austrian, and English origins. They worked as gandy dancers, railroaders, sheep or cattle men, miners, loggers, trappers, carpenters, and prospectors. Occasionally there was an itinerant preacher.

The shoemaker was a small elfinlike man with a name to match—Fowinkle. He actually made shoes for people, softening the leather that he cut from a hide in a large wooden tub, then sewing the shoes together. We kids loved to watch him work. He didn't seem to mind, but he never talked much. Our conversations were limited to one question and one answer.

"What do you do that for?" the kids would ask him.

1906 photo of the Tolland, Colorado, cafe and post office on the newly constructed Denver, Northwestern Pacific Railway. Postmaster Elizabeth Clifton, sitting.

"Cat fur to make kitten britches" was his vexing reply.

The monotony of it all got to Fowinkle occasionally. He would walk the mile to Baltimore for a visit to Hatfield's saloon. One night as he was coming home he failed to make a turn in the road and walked right through a shallow lake near town. When kidded by grown-ups about this, he would never admit walking through the lake. He explained to his wife that he had come through "one hell of a rainstorm." She reminded him that it had been a clear night. The whiskey from Hatfield's kegs had authority! The lake

7

henceforth became known as Shoemaker Lake. No one else in our town ever had anything named for him.

Schoolteachers came and went, sometimes as many as three in one term. Most of the population in towns like this were male, either single or away from their families. Consequently there were never many children in school. The schoolhouse was typical: white with a belfry housing a large school bell. If there happened to be an itinerant preacher in town, church was held in the schoolhouse.

Our town had higher education too. There was a summer branch of the University of Colorado, where alpine flora and fauna were studied. There were more college kids than grade school kids in town. Dr. Francis Ramaley, who was dean of the biology department at the university, conducted the classes.

At the Saturday-night dances, Dr. Ramaley would be called upon to tell a story during intermission. One of our favorites was about frogs in the village lake. He would accentuate his story with "ribbet, ribbet," imitating the various frogs in his tale and changing the inflection to identify their age and sex.

Sheep and cattle men who ran their stock in the nearby hills where the alpine forage was nutritious needed a stockyard and loading pen in order to ship their stock by rail. One was built west of town. We kids loved to watch the sheepmen load sheep into the railroad cars. The men would drag the first sheep up the chute bodily, and then all the others would follow in a mad rush to get aboard the sheep car.

People in Denver needed ice, and J. Reimer Espy began cutting ice during the winters on Park Lake. He built an ice-storage house, then shipped the ice to Denver in boxcars during the summers. Watching the men cut and put up ice in the winter was a special joy.

Important news and events, such as the Jess Willard–Jack Dempsey heavyweight championship fight, came in over the telegraph at the railroad depot. Most of the town's hundred or so men packed into the depot lobby to listen to the telegrapher translate the clatter of Morse code into a blow-by-blow description. This was one of the really big nights in town, and it was free.

Boulder Park also has a lost gold mine. The evasive lode is called the Whistling Jack, as enchanting a name as many another lost bonanza. As the story goes, an old prospector by the name of Whistling Jack had a log cabin located west of Tolland before the railroad came into the park. Unlike most prospectors, his wife lived with him. Every few weeks Whistling Jack and his wife would take provisions for several days and steal away in the night. When they would return—again late at night—they would have a large poke of gold. No one seemed to know what eventually happened to Whistling Jack and his wife. They disappeared and never returned. Their gold mine was supposed to be located near what was later called Dead Man's Gulch, but no trace of either Whistling Jack, his wife, or the gold source has ever been found.

But the Whistling Jack lode is still there for discovery. There were always skeptics around town who suspected that Whistling Jack and his wife may have been "high-grading" the gold at night from some miner's sluice box over in Russell Gulch. Maybe they were caught on one of their trips and so could be in the bottom of any one of hundreds of abandoned mine shafts, far from Dead Man's Gulch. But thoughts like that are not nearly as fascinating as a lost gold mine called the Whistling Jack; I want to believe it's still there.

In the 1920s, Dr. Edward Uhlenhuth of the Rockefeller Institute in New York came to Tolland in search of a thing far different from gold or the Whistling Jack. He came to collect high-altitude salamanders, which he found in Shoemaker and Park lakes. He would catch them and put them in half-gallon galvanized beer buckets fitted with press-down lids. Each day he would take several cans of salamanders to the depot and send them Railway Express to New York on the evening train. This seemed to disturb depot agent John Scandlan, who complained that the doctor always brought his "damned polliwogs" into the express office just before the train was due. The doctor argued that he wanted the salamanders to be as fresh as possible for their two thousand mile trip to New York.

Regardless of his difficulties, Dr. Uhlenhuth helped find something more precious than gold. Studies conducted on the specimens he sent to New York later led to the discovery of iodine as a treatment for certain thyroid conditions and goiter trouble.

Besides the dances held when the excursion picnics came to town, there was the usual village Saturday-night dance. People had to make their own fun. Two young men, Albert Luke and Hans Mosch, both good at playing the mouth organ, furnished music for the Saturday-night dances. Several young people learned to waltz while listening to the harmonica music played by Luke and Mosch, who were usually accompanied by one of the ladies who could play the piano.

A favorite form of amusement was the nightly gathering at the general merchandise store, which by 1915 was owned by my father and Edward S. Evans, my uncle. The firm, Clifton & Evans, sold everything from coal-oil lamps to miners' acetylene lamps. The store had the only telephone in town and housed mother's post office. Dad was the notary public, and Evans did the local hauling, which included anything from a wagon load of lumber to a cake of ice. No one could get his mail, make a telephone call, or close a legal deal without coming into our store. Competition was almost nonexistent.

Around the potbellied stove near the rear of the store opposite the post office section the men gathered in the evening. There were chairs and stools and occasionally a cider barrel. The only thing missing from the traditional country-store scene was the cracker barrel. The competitive discussions were good and usually educational, particularly for a young boy. In addition to acquiring the vocabulary of a professional mule skinner, one could absorb a smattering of Mexican Spanish; learn about railroading, logging, and mining; and learn how to shear a sheep or shoe a horse—all depending on who happened to be in town on a given night. It was the answer to today's television and Rotary, Kiwanis, or Lion's clubs. And it was well attended.

In season, politics was a favorite, and frequently a hot, subject. Dad was a staunch Democrat, and his partner Evans was as equally strong a Republican. They learned early never to get into arguments about politics. Before elections, there was a sort of truce. The store was split down the center lengthwise according to party sympathy. Clifton stayed on one side, Evans stayed on the other. The Republican candidates left their literature on the right as you entered the store; the Democrats left theirs on the left, which somehow seemed to be the proper side for them.

The gasoline automobile didn't reach our town until about the summer of 1916, when a Chevrolet arrived. It was not because the town was isolated; it was simply because the automobile in those days had trouble pulling up the steep grades to reach Tolland. The driver of the car came into the store to buy some gasoline because he was almost out. There was no gasoline in town—even at Clifton & Evans, where you could buy almost everything. The driver had to settle for a couple gallons of kerosene. We called it coal oil, and everyone in town used it for their table lamps. The kerosene did get the Chevrolet on its way out of town, leaving behind it a dense cloud of black exhaust as a harbinger of things to come.

A Stanley Steamer was the first rubber-tired horseless carriage to reach our town; it, too, arrived in 1916. This car had been built by the owner of the Stanley Hotel, in nearby Estes Park, to bring tourists from Denver to his hotel.

When I reached the age of fifteen, I could work in the post office. For fifteen dollars a month I carted the mail between the post office and the depot, meeting the two mail trains. The mail trains carried a railway mail car, and a railway mail clerk distributed mail between towns.

We had an old bay horse named Bill, who was once part of the team Uncle Ed used to haul groceries and freight. After considerable scrounging, I was able to get some wagon wheels and a one-horse whiffletree. I built a four-wheeled wagon and patched together some harness for old Bill. I painted the wagon green and printed ZIP on the side, with an arrow through the letters. In addition to hauling the mail, I picked up extra work by hauling baggage and suitcases for tourists who came to town for summer vacations. There was other light hauling to be done around town— garbage, coal, and firewood. The operation really had no zip, for old Bill was sixteen years old and had his own pace. Our town probably had the first zip in the postal service, far, far ahead of its time.

One day something new came in the mail. It was a circular to be posted on the outside of the post office. It announced a reward of over fourteen thousand dollars for the arrest and conviction of three men wanted for the holdup of a mail train. During the holdup, the brakeman, engineer, fireman, and railway mail clerk had all been killed. It was a shocking cold-blooded operation.

I had met many of the mail clerks who worked on the trains that went through our town. Being raised in a railroad town, I knew that trainmen sometimes died in train wrecks or accidents. It was hard to believe a railway mail clerk had been shot.

The wanted circular fascinated me, and I would look at it often and wonder how they could ever catch the three men. Most of all, I wondered how the post office inspectors had ever been able to find out who had committed the crime and how they had become sure enough to print such a circular. They actually had pictures of the three on the circular, although there were no witnesses to the holdup and the three had slipped away after the holdup into the Siskiyou Mountains.

That the case was ever solved is to the credit of hardworking investigators and scientific analysis. Most of the facts came from unrelated shreds of evidence carefully and tediously collected.

The holdup had occurred at Tunnel 13 on October 11, 1923, on the Southern Pacific line in the Siskiyou Mountains of Oregon. On that day, three young men took dynamite about thirty feet inside the south entrance of the tunnel on their last step in a long-planned mail train robbery.

One man stayed with the dynamite and the detonating machine while two others went to the north entrance of the tunnel, where they would board the engine as it slowed to test the airbrakes before the train entered the tunnel and began its descent into California.

The holdup had proceeded according to the plan of the three, but met with failure all around. As adroit detective work would later prove, the three responsible were brothers, Roy, Ray, and Hugh DeAutremont. When the train slowed, Hugh jumped into the engine cab and Roy climbed onto the back tender. Ray had stayed at the south end of the tunnel with the dynamite.

They stopped the train just before it emerged from the tunnel. The railway mail clerk, apparently wondering why the train had stopped, stuck his head out the side door of the mail car. Ray fired a shotgun blast at him when he wouldn't open up, but apparently he missed. The dynamite was then placed against the front door of the mail car and set off. This filled the tunnel with considerable smoke and started a fire in the mail car. The three then tried to uncouple the mail car from the rest of the train so that it could be moved, but because of the smoke they were unable to manage it.

Rear brakeman Coyle Johnson walked forward to see why the train wasn't moving, and when he reached the head end he was shot by both Ray and Hugh. Finding they couldn't get inside the mail car, they shot the fireman and the engineer of the train. The railway mail clerk was burned to death in the fire in the mail car. The three DeAutremonts then gave up and vanished empty-handed.

Post Office Inspectors Hougen and Brunner were among the first to reach the scene. Their search of the area turned up a tramp who reported seeing two men in overalls board the train before it entered the tunnel. A search of the tracks turned up a .45 caliber Colt revolver and a DuPont detonator with insulated wire running from it to the spot where the mail car had been blown up.

Not far distant were pieces of gunnysack soaked in creosote, which had obviously been used to prevent bloodhounds from being able to trail the men. Three packsacks were found near the discarded creosote foot pads. These had apparently been intended to be used to carry away the loot. Before nightfall hundreds of men scoured the region. Bloodhounds were brought in to trail the holdup men, and airplanes searched from above. A company of Oregon militia was put into action to aid in searching the vast mountain region for the men.

Combing the area turned up two campsites and a small cabin where the bandits had stayed for three days prior to the holdup attempt. Every possible piece of evidence was picked up and carefully preserved, including a traveling bag with a shipping tag pasted on it. Odd as it may seem, it was later found that the most-important piece of evidence was a pair of greasy blue-denim overalls that were picked up near the scene of the crime.

The search continued for days. Numerous suspects were questioned to no avail. At this point about all that was learned was the fact that three unknown men had taken part in the holdup. The only witnesses who had taken a good look at the men were dead.

The overalls seemed to hold some kind of clue, but several detectives failed to come up with anything. This being in the days before the postal inspector crime laboratory, it was finally decided to send all physical evidence to Edward O. Heinrich. Heinrich was a chemist at the University of California who had gained some recognition as a scientific analyst in crime detection.

In due time the post office inspectors had a call from Heinrich, who surprised them by the amazing completeness of his analysis. Heinrich reported, "One of the men you are looking for is a left-handed lumberjack who has worked in the Northwest recently. He is about twenty-six, has brown hair, weighs about 165 pounds, stands five foot eight inches tall, and he's rather fastidious in his personal habits."

When questioned about how he arrived at this deduction, he said, "There are streaks of fresh pitch in the overalls that could have gotten there only through contact with pine trees. This suggests that the man is a lumberjack. I found Douglas Fir needles in the pockets, which places him in the Northwest. A few strands of hair on the overalls tells me his hair color and also determines his approximate age. There were worn places on the right side of the overalls but none on the left, so our man must have been standing with his right side against a tree while he swung his ax."

The clincher came when Heinrich said, "I believe his name is Roy DeAutremont. I discovered a little piece of faded yellow paper jammed down in the narrow pencil pocket of the overalls. There appeared to be no writing on it, but under a microscope I detected some faint pen scratches. I brought them out under treatment in the laboratory."

Heinrich found that the scrap of paper was a receipt for a

registered letter mailed by Roy DeAutremont at Eugene, Oregon, on September 14, 1923. It bore number 236-L, and showed that fifty dollars had been sent on that date to Hugh DeAutremont in Lakewood, New Mexico.

A Paul DeAutremont was turned up in Eugene, Oregon. He was found to be a peaceful law-abiding barber who never left town. When interviewed, he said he had three sons—Roy and Ray, both twenty-six, and Hugh, eighteen. The father said that Hugh had been going to high school in Lakewood, New Mexico. When he was graduated he came to Oregon to join his brothers, who worked as lumberjacks near Silverton, Oregon. Paul said that Roy was left-handed, bearing out Heinrich's deductions. The father turned over all the personal effects the boys left before they disappeared.

Heinrich continued to turn up valuable information. Only three digits had been legible on the .45 caliber Colt found at the holdup scene. Heinrich located the full set under the top strap of the revolver frame. The gun was finally traced to Seattle, where it had been sold to a man who signed the name William Elliot. Handwriting analysis determined that the Elliot signature was actually that of Roy DeAutremont. The express tag on the bag found near the tracks showed that Roy DeAutremont had shipped the bag from Portland, Oregon, to Eugene, Oregon, on January 21, 1923.

The web of evidence continued to mount, pointing more conclusively to the three DeAutremont brothers; but they could not be found. The Southern Pacific Railroad and the Post Office Department both offered rewards. The post office inspectors had over two million reward posters printed and placed in the lobby of every post office in the country. Many were printed in Spanish, German, French, Dutch, or Portuguese and sent to the far corners of the world. The posters reached police and sheriff officers, military posts, and organizations or business places where the DeAutremonts might be known.

The first wanted circulars were issued in 1923, but it was three years before a break came. In the meantime, hours, days, and weeks were spent in monotonous running down of tips and false leads. The DeAutremonts seemed to have vanished from the earth.

15

Finally, Thomas Reynolds, a corporal in the army who had been stationed in the Philippines, walked into the post office inspector's office in San Francisco and reported he had recognized the picture of Hugh DeAutremont on a wanted circular. He said he had served with the man in the Philippines and that he was going under the name of Jim Price.

Hugh DeAutremont, alias Jim Price, was arrested in Manila and readily admitted being the long-sought Hugh. He denied any knowledge of the Siskiyou Mountain train holdup. He was brought back to Oregon and charged with first-degree murder.

Hugh's arrest gained wide publicity in the press, and in far away Portsmouth, Ohio, Albert Collingsworth, a partially blind man, recognized pictures of Roy and Ray DeAutremont as two men he had worked with. They were going under the names of Clarence and Elmer Goodwin. These two were arrested, and both admitted being the DeAutremont twins, but they, too, denied being implicated in the mail train holdup.

Hugh was tried first, and cross-examination of the prosecution's main witness, Edward Heinrich, failed to discredit his findings. Hugh was found guilty, but the jurors spared his life. Encouraged, Roy and Ray pled guilty. All three were sentenced to life imprisonment. It was said that the four-year investigation cost the Post Office Department, the Southern Pacific Railroad, and the Railway Express nearly a half million dollars to bring the DeAutremonts to justice.

One of the post office inspectors who worked long and hard on the case was Tennyson Jefferson. The name fascinated me. Those days of my youth generated a desire to be able to ride on trains and investigate interesting criminal cases. I wanted to be a post office inspector. My parents had always seemed to hold post office inspectors in high esteem. In fact, they were always particular about how they operated the post office.

Tolland was no place for a young man to make much of a living. The Moffat Tunnel was completed in 1929, and trains then went under, instead of over, the Continental Divide. This meant that there was no longer a need for helper engines or rotary snowplows.

Unlike others across the West, our town had started to die. Mining had long since been given up. Most of the timber had been logged off and shipped out. Only the sheep and cattle men remained, along with a dwindling number of old-timers. My dad sold the store.

It was really time to leave. Dr. Ramaley and my mother decided it would be a good idea for me to go to the university. This may have been the best decision anyone ever made for me.

In the fall of 1927, I left Tolland, taking the train to a little whistle-stop called Scenic. From there I walked, carrying a suitcase, down the mountain and across the flats. I caught the Interurban to University Station in Boulder. It was to be a long time before I would be given my first post office inspector commission.

2

Pioneer Alaskan Mail Routes

"FEEDING AT THE PUBLIC TROUGH!"

This epithet was hurled at me by a disgruntled and probably hungry old man on a Denver street corner, where I was defenselessly loading a mail bag and preparing to deliver mail on my first day on a new job. It was October 1, 1935.

I shall never forget the remark. Possibly it was a defiant gesture against all bureaucracy, which was then really only in its infancy. Although I didn't realize it, I was starting on the ground floor in a profession that was to prosper fantastically, government service! It didn't seem too promising at that particular time. I had just finished studying engineering for five years and had a degree to prove it. Along the way, I had taken a civil service examination for mail clerk-carrier, along with about five thousand other depression job seekers in April 1930. I was able to work during Christmas rush periods at the Denver post office while I was attending college. Now, after five years, my name had inched to the top of the eligible list, and I was called to work as a substitute letter carrier.

It was a good job for the times. I received $0.65 an hour to start, which was more than the $14.50 a week I had been making as a chemical engineer under the National Recovery Act (NRA).

I quickly learned that having one's nose in the government feed bag wasn't a soft touch insofar as the Post Office Department was concerned. As a letter carrier, one had the mail on his back all day,

18

and one had only one way to get rid of it: deliver it. The work was interesting, healthy, and tension free. It was natural that I would become active in the National Association of Letter Carriers, and in a few years I was elected secretary of Branch 47 in Denver.

In the course of time I met most of the leaders in the National Association of Letter Carriers, including James K. Langan of Pittston, Pennsylvania, who always gave me advice, counsel, and direction. I attended a caucus at the Los Angeles convention, which led to the election of Bill Doherty as president of the NALC.

All of this was intriguing, but I was interested in travel and I wanted to investigate interesting criminal cases. I wanted to see more of the world—other places, even foreign lands. I believed that post office inspectors must do all those things.

As I became more serious, I began to make inquiries about how a letter carrier obtained the position of post office inspector. I soon found that an applicant had to have five years of postal service and be between the ages twenty-five and thirty-five. He must also be able to pass a very stiff civil service examination covering general subjects, post office accounting, and postal laws and regulations. There was also a tough physical examination. I wanted the job so much I started studying in the face of what seemed an almost hopeless battle.

As soon as I had spent the necessary five years carrying mail, I wrote a letter to the chief post office inspector, asking that I be given an examination for the position of post office inspector. Eventually I had a call from Post Office Inspector Martin Wenger, who gave me a day-long examination of his own, just to see if I might be able to pass the civil service examination and otherwise measure up to the standards of the time. It was said the post office inspectors picked their own company. Wenger interviewed my neighbors, my prior places of employment, old friends, old enemies, schools, the corner grocer, and then made a surprise visit to my home, where he talked to my wife alone. His investigation was as thorough as a national security clearance check.

When he had finished, he told me he would recommend that I be given the examination. The civil service examination required the better part of two days, and I found it difficult. After I had passed, I was sent for a thorough physical examination. When it was all over, nothing happened for nine long months.

Post office inspectors of that time carried a small three-by-five-inch heavy leather-covered credential called a commission. One of the happiest days of my life was the day I received mine, delivered by registered mail.

The commission was dated October 5, 1942, and it read, "Robert B. Clifton, post office inspector, is a duly accredited agent or officer of this department and travels by my direction on its business. He will be obeyed and respected accordingly by mail contractors, postmasters, and all others connected with the postal service. Railroads, steamboats, stages, and other mail contractors are required to extend the facilities of free travel to the holder of this commission." It was signed by Frank C. Walker, postmaster general.

To me it was pretty heady reading, and I was justifiably proud. It is a shame the commissions do not read the same today. If they did, we would probably enjoy better mail service. I was now in a business where the responsibilities were great, the work interesting and challenging. The post office had always maintained a high standard of honesty and integrity, both in accounting and in the way it handled the mail of the public.

My job was to be the eyes and ears of the postmaster general. Reports to him had to be honest, factual, and uncolored. Recommendations were made without fear of political or other repercussions. After schooling in Washington, D.C., I was sent to the Pacific Northwest for further training. The first assignment that was totally my own, after six months of training, took me to Whitehorse, Yukon Territory, Canada, where I began a military assignment that extended from Edmonton, Alberta, to Nome, Alaska, and as far north as Norman Wells in Canada's Northwest Territories. From Whitehorse I flew to Edmonton and then north to Norman Wells.

I could hardly say my dreams about being a postal inspector had been wrong. In little more than a year I had been on trains, a steamship, and an airplane; and I had seen several states and was traveling in a foreign land.

I was launched on an interesting career, the first part of which was spent in Alaska. During some of this time, I was the only postal inspector in Alaska and traveled almost constantly. In the mid 1940s, it was my happy experience to fly with some of those great pioneer arctic bush pilots who forged together the bush airmail routes. True, there were more hours spent waiting than flying, but the hours passed in "hangar flying," when pilots would gather to wait out bad weather and regale one another with tall stories of their flying experiences. Flying schedules were "Weather Permitting" and "Pilot Willing," or WP and PW. All bush flying was under visual flight rules, or VFR, and those pilots who lived to fly another day had to be both careful and capable. At that, far too many were lost.

It seemed that almost every early winter, November or December, some mail plane somewhere in Alaska would fail to make a trip. Flying in February and March was not as treacherous. Then the weather was not subject to the sudden changes that frequently occurred earlier. It was more likely to be clear but colder. By then the ground was well padded with snow.

When one had to fly, it was better to fly with a pilot who had at least ten years of experience flying the north. Two of the very best were Sig and Noel Wien. Neither did much hangar flying, but they really knew their business. They specialized in the arctic, flying over some of the roughest, coldest, and most-deserted land in the world.

I suppose Sig Wien logged more flights north of the Arctic Circle than any pilot before transcontinental polar flights. I once flew with Sig from Wiseman, seventy miles north of the Arctic Circle, to Fairbanks. That was on April 3, 1946, and we landed on the Yukon River at Steven's Village to pick up a passenger. A few miles downstream from there was where the first bridge was built across the Yukon in 1974. There were no roads or airstrips when we made that trip, but it was as smooth as silk, both in the air and during the landings.

A year later, on March 11 to 12, 1947, Noel Wien was testing a new Stinson 120. He agreed to take me to Jack Wade, Chicken, and Eagle up in the Forty-mile Country of northeast Alaska. Audits were overdue at Chicken and Eagle. The post office at Jack Wade had been closed for the winter, but the key that opened mail pouches had not been turned in. These keys would open any mail pouch in the United States, and the Inspection Service became uneasy when one was unaccounted for.

Noel Wien had flown mining equipment into the old mining camp of Jack Wade in the late 1930s, using a Tri-Motor Ford. To give you an idea of the precautions this man took, half the load on the small Stinson we were to fly was survival equipment. Some of the men kidded him while helping him load a primus stove, sleeping bags, snowshoes, an SOS radio, K rations, a tent, and plenty of provisions. Noel, who never did talk much, just went ahead methodically getting ready. If we had been forced down, we would have been self-sufficient for a month.

About sixty miles out of Fairbanks the radio contact was lost. This didn't bother Noel; he had flown many years without a radio. It was a nice clear day, we were warm inside the heated cabin of the plane, and the scenery was spectacular, with many ice-capped peaks rising over five thousand feet.

Noel flew into Jack Wade just as he had done years before in the Tri-Motor, through a low pass between some mountains and then sharply down onto the field. The clearing was still there, but now the field was just a large flat area covered with several feet of powdered snow. It was a little late to "pull up," so he landed. The ski plane came to a stop, and out of the silent white wilderness came a lone sourdough on snowshoes, delighted to see someone— anyone. He gave us the traditional Alaskan's welcome: "Come on over to my shack for coffee."

He had been alone for about four months, having decided to stay over the winter in the bush. Noel didn't think we really had time for coffee; it was after 3:00 P.M. and darkness would come early. We had to tramp out a runway in the soft snow, or the plane would never get off.

One of the last pictures taken (1935) of Will Rogers and Wiley Post on the Chena River at Fairbanks just before they took off for Barrow, Alaska, where they crashed and lost their lives. Left to right, Will Rogers, Leonhard Seppala, Wiley Post and bush pilot Joe Crossen.

Where was the Jack Wade Post Office building? The sourdough said it was up the creek about seven miles—it kept moving along with the miners as they worked the placer ground. It had been perhaps ten years since Noel had first flown into Jack Wade.

Did the sourdough know anything about the mailbox key? No. He didn't even know where the post office might have been when it was closed for the winter. Any thought of trying to find the missing key was quickly abandoned. Looking for a key in a nonexistent floating post office seemed the least of our problems at the time.

Noel recruited the sourdough to help, and we all put on snowshoes and went to work beating down the snow so that the plane could get off. The task was fairly well completed to Noel's satisfaction by dusk. The two of us got into the plane, and the miner held onto the tail while Noel revved it up. Then, when he could hang on no longer, he let go, getting a blast of powdered snow in his face for the courtesy. We made a fast run down the newly packed runway and were soon airborne.

It was only a few minutes flying time to Chicken, where the icy landing strip seemed to be built on the side of a canyon at a twenty-degree angle. It was getting dark, but Noel brought the Stinson in on all the proper angles, which was not unusual for him, although he had lost the sight of one eye years before.

Was the mail key at Jack Wade ever found? Yes, under a cookbook in a wanigan after the ice breakup the next spring, when the miners came back to moil for gold.

Noel Wien has been honored many times in later years for his devotion to pioneer bush flying. His most cherished honor was being named to the OX-5 Club's Aviation Hall of Fame in 1972. On November 19, 1974, Noel was made the seventh honorary member of the Airline Pilot's Association. The other six were Orville Wright, W. A. Patterson, Will Rogers, Eddie Ricken-backer, Jimmy Doolittle, and Charles A. Lindberg. Noel passed away in retirement July 18, 1977, in Bellevue, Washington.

Col. Carl Ben Eielson is considered to be the father of Alaskan aviation and certainly the father of Alaskan airmail. At the age of twenty-five he came to Fairbanks, Alaska, as a mathematics

Carl Ben Eielson, a Fairbanks, Alaska school teacher advocate of the airplane as a solution to Alaska's need for some better medium of transportation. He flew the first air mail in Alaska, Fairbanks to McGrath, in 3 hours as against the 20 days it took the dog team. Plane was loaned by the Post Office Department. The plane was later wrecked. Eielson Field (AFB), 26 miles from Fairbanks, was named in his honor. He lost his life in an attempted air rescue of furs in Siberia.

teacher in the high school. But his mind was not always on teaching. He dreamed of flying the barren desolate expanse of interior Alaska. He could visualize what aerial traffic would mean to the isolated people living in the small scattered villages in a roadless territory that was thinly crisscrossed by dog-team trails.

Eielson finally prevailed upon the Post Office Department to furnish him with a DeHavilland plane for an experiment to determine if it would be practical to transport winter mail in Alaska by air instead of by dog team. No flights had ever been made under such adverse arctic conditions.

On February 21, 1924, Eielson flew the mail from Fairbanks to McGrath in three hours over territory that required about ten days by dogsled. This was well over two years before the first mail was officially flown under contract in the "lower forty-eight" states. Unfortunately, the DeHavilland later was wrecked, and the Post Office Department refused to replace it.

After his historic flight, Eielson went on to act as pilot for arctic explorer Sir Hubert Wilkins. After two years of exploratory flights north of Point Barrow, the northernmost point of land in the United States, the two flew two thousand two hundred miles from Barrow to Spitzbergen in 1928. Later they made air flights into the Antarctic.

Returning to Alaska in 1929, Eielson entered commercial flying. His first opportunity came when the steamer *Nanuk* became icebound in Siberian waters and her owners offered fifty thousand dollars for the rescue of the million dollars in furs that were aboard the American-owned vessel. The first load was brought back in October.

On the following trip, Eielson and Borland left Teller, Alaska, on November 9, 1929, following bush pilot Frank Dorbandt and mechanic Bud Bassett. Dorbandt and Bassett later turned back because of bad weather, but Eielson and Borland continued on to disappear in the vast Arctic.

Among the first to begin a search were bush pilots Joe Crosson and Harold Gillam. Although many participated during subsequent days, those two stuck it out for seventy-two days whenever it was possible to fly. Finally, on January 26, 1930, Crosson was rewarded by catching the glitter reflected by part of a wing tip of Eielson's lost plane which was buried in the snow near the Siberian coastline. Gillam was flying close by.

During the search Crosson and Gillam were frequently separated, sometimes lost, as they flew up and down the valleys on the coast of Siberia. When Crosson noticed the wing of the Eielson plane, he and Gillam were able to land near the wreckage. The Hamilton had been completely destroyed, and both Eielson and Borland thrown clear, their bodies buried in snow.

A dog team was dispatched from the *Nanuk*, and five men were flown to the wreck from Cape North to assist in digging for the bodies. Three days later two junkers, piloted by Russians, arrived to assist in the work. Borland's body was found February 13, and Eielson was found February 18. The bodies were flown back to Alaska by the Russians.

Both Crosson and Gillam were well equipped for arctic weather during their search. They carried sleeping bags, primus stoves, and enough food to last for weeks. Crosson was flying a Waco with a Whirlwind motor, and Gillam flew a Stearman. Their search was made during some of the shortest days in the year, when daylight lasted only about four hours in that part of the far north. There is little growth in the Arctic, and when the earth is entirely covered with snow, it is extremely difficult to distinguish landmarks. Cliffs along the shorelines do provide a landmark, and houses—where there were any—appeared black, but it was necessary to fly very low to see the Siberian Chuchi huts. Temperatures ranged from thirty to fifty degrees below zero Fahrenheit, and the speed of the open-cockpit planes added a substantial chill factor.

After the pioneering of Eielson and others, arctic air travel flourished. By the 1940s, airplanes were fast becoming the accepted way to move mail, freight, and people in Alaska. By the end of the 1940s, only two dogsled routes remained. Even so, flying mail to the many small villages was no easy task. Almost every landing on the crudely built small fields, on river bars, ocean beaches, or glaciers were what many would today call a forced landing. In the winter, when everything was covered with snow, landings with ski planes were not as hazardous and could be made on frozen lakes and rivers. The pilots of that day did it for a living, and many still do.

After Eielson's airmail flight in 1924, nothing was done by the Post Office Department about air service in Alaska until 1928, when Noel Wien was given a contract to fly five hundred pounds of mail from Fairbanks to Nome on three trips during the spring ice breakup, when no mail was normally moved. Performance was mandatory, and future contracts would be lost if flights were not made on schedule. Noel made the first two flights, and the third was made by his brother Ralph under great difficulty, because he had only a few hours of flying time and was sick at the time. The flights were successful, and the beginning of a vast airmail network in Alaska was born.

In the 1940s, bush pilot Frank Barr, well known by the people along the Kuskokwim River, was flying the mail to small villages on the river using a Pilgrim on wheels. Often he would be unable to land at some of the villages, and the mail would be brought on into Bethel. Bush pilot Don Emmons was to take a Travelaire on floats from Bethel to Anchorage for its one thousand-hour overhaul. Barr asked him to drop off mail that had been missed, which Don could do because the landings could be made on the river by the floatplane. I wanted to audit the small post offices, so I went along.

Don had been flying in Alaska since 1930, and I had flown with him before. Don had never put a scratch on any airplane he had flown, but on this trip I once felt we were going to put on much more than a mere scratch. The motor was performing poorly. Every time Don started to take off from the river, water would splash up onto the motor and it would cough and miss. After we left Napaimut, Don decided to take a shortcut over the mountains because we didn't need to land at Crooked Creek.

Along the way, the engine suddenly sputtered and quit entirely. That was a moment I'll always remember. We looked down for a place to land. The thin gray line of the river, the only possible place to land, seemed to me much too far away for any glide.

Good old Don teased the motor and, remarkably, got it going again. His two other passengers and I simultaneously started to live again. He turned down toward the river and then followed it up to Sleetmute, where he beached the plane across the river from the village. We found an old abandoned schoolhouse where we stayed all night. I had been carrying an arctic sleeping bag with me on all flights for months, never using it. That night it came in handy and justified all the bother it had been.

The following day Don worked on the motor until early afternoon and, after getting it running fairly well, decided to abort the trip. We flew back downriver to Bethel, glad to get back.

I always thought Don Emmons must have been a remarkable pilot, because they gave him some real junk to fly—planes other pilots would refuse to go up in. A few years after our Kuskokwim trip, he gave up flying, only to later lose his life after twenty years of dangerous bush flying in a pulp-mill accident in Ketchikan.

Northern Cross was the enchanting name of an airline operated by John Cross out of Kotzebue. On November 8, 1946, I flew with John from Nome to investigate the crash of a small bush plane carrying mail somewhere near Kotzebue Sound. Because November was never my choice as a good month for arctic flying, I was probably a little apprehensive. There had been a fairly bad storm at Nome, and we delayed three days before starting the trip.

John Cross was not new to arctic flying. He had previously flown for Wien Airlines out of Fairbanks and had been commanding officer at Naknek Air Base during the war. On this trip he introduced me to a condition called a whiteout. Of course, the flying was contact, which meant that the pilot navigated by visually checking his course with known landmarks.

When we left Nome, the weather was cloudy and the temperature was about thirty degrees below zero Fahrenheit. After being airborne about thirty minutes, we were flying through air where everything appeared white. The fog in the cold temperature had crystallized. It was eerie—like being suspended inside a huge, white balloon. Many pilots have encountered difficulty under such conditions, not uncommon in the early winter months.

Another bush pilot had left Nome at about the same time as we, and for a while we could see him flying along the same course about a thousand feet to our right. When we entered the whiteout, we lost sight of his plane but continued to wonder how far from us he might be. We later learned he had turned back. John Cross was living at Deering on the south shore of Kotzebue Sound at the time, and I presume he was anxious to get home after being weather-bound in Nome for several days. At any rate, we kept on going, although it was about an hour's flying time to Deering.

Luckily John knew the country and the location of the mountains along the way. He was heading for the arctic shoreline, where he hoped to pick up some landmark to regain visual control. It seemed like an extremely long flight before he sighted the black jagged outline of the coast cliffs, a very welcome sight. After this it was simple; he just followed the coastline east to Deering. When we landed, it had started to snow heavily. We couldn't go on toward Kotzebue for three days.

The previous fall I had to make a trip to Shishmaref to investigate a mail-tampering case in the same general area. At the time bush pilot Frank Whaley, who had started flying out of Nome in the early 1930s, was flying for Wien. I made arrangements for him to fly me from Nome to Shishmaref. He was flying a Gullwing Stinson on wheels and landed on the sandy beach in front of the village.

The investigation took only a few hours, but that was too long to avoid one of those sudden storms that come out of the Arctic in the fall. Frank headed the plane into the coming storm, and several of the local Eskimo helped tie it down to planking on the beach, which was stacked with sacks of coal borrowed from the native schoolhouse nearby. Frank was taking no chances of the plane being airborne or blown about by the approaching storm.

Shishmaref on October 25, 1945, was a village of about two hundred Eskimo, a Lutheran missionary and his wife, a schoolteacher and his wife, and the local trader. While it may not seem much of a problem, there was no place to stay unless one accepted the hospitality of one of the residents. Everybody wanted us to stay with them—the preacher, the teacher, and the trader. In isolated villages like Shishmaref, the residents have little opportunity to visit with anyone from outside the village, and outside gossip is a pleasant respite from the monotony of local visiting.

The missionaries, Mr. and Mrs. Dahle, had a shortwave radio, and the pilot felt that we should stay with them because there we could be informed of current weather reports.

Our visit lasted six days before the storm abated, a period when no bush planes flew, except one. We listened on the radio when Archie Ferguson took off from nearby Kotzebue with his usual staccato chatter with the CAA tower there. After he took off, the operator at the field announced, "No one else is flying, but Archie just took off for the Kobuk. With this wind, he could be in Kiana in a few minutes. His departure was routine; he knocked over several oil drums at the end of the field as he left."

The six days spent with the Lutheran missionaries passed swiftly. We divided our time between listening to the radio, reading, and

Bush pilot Frank Whaley of Nome, Alaska, shown with Eskimo helpers lashing down the Gullwing Stinson mail plane before a storm at Shishmaref. Schoolhouse in background (October 1945).

talking to the Dahles. We attended an Eskimo wedding in the Lutheran church and visited many Eskimo families, including George Ahgupuk, the famous Eskimo artist, whose home was at Shisharef. Ahgupuk was then becoming famous for his sketches on bleached reindeer hide, all of which are priceless today.

After five days, the missionary decided we needed a bath—a strange idea in a land where it is said no one bathes during the six-month winters. However, he may have thought we needed a little exercise, or perhaps they wanted us out of the house for a few hours. He set us to cutting ice with an ice saw on a nearby lake. An Eskimo boy with a five-dog team hauled the ice to the house, where it was placed in a large galvanized tub on the stove to melt. We learned that it takes an unbelievable amount of ice to make enough water for a bath, and before we had enough for the Dahles and us, the weather cleared and we left, still unbathed in the true tradition of the Arctic.

One of the cases we had in those days was partially solved in an unusual way. We had help from the fox and wolf. In old Alaska, the trappers and traders would tell you that the fox will scent out and curiously investigate any unusual or foreign matter that may be hidden under the arctic snow. Strange as it may seem, following animal tracks through the snow once helped us locate a cache of stolen mail.

It was Christmas 1947, and the children of the Kenai peninsula south of Anchorage just hadn't received many of the very precious Christmas parcels they expected. Complaints were heard from Ninilchik, Kasilof, and Kenai.

Where was the missing mail? It had apparently left Anchorage, and it seemed unlikely there could be a mail thief at every one of the small villages. The mail was taken from the Anchorage post office to Merrill Field, where a bush plane would fly it south once a week to the villages. At that time there was no highway or road to Ninilchik or Kasilof. Many possibilities for theft were considered. Could the mail be disappearing at Merrill Field or even before it left the Anchorage post office? Was the bush plane flying it to some secret cache out in the vast tundra where an accomplice was waiting? Was it being stolen between the Anchorage post office and Merrill Field?

Inspector Carl A. Hoyer and I were given the case. Our investigation at Merrill Field finally centered on the Eskimo caretaker for the airline that flew the mail. He also drove the company truck. He lived alone in the airline office in a small room adjacent to where mail was stored before it was flown out. He seemed a logical suspect, and some damaging evidence of rifled mail was found in his quarters, but he was not one to talk freely and would admit no guilt.

The few items he had sequestered in his small quarters were far from the volume of mail reported missing. Did he have accomplices, and where was the missing mail? There was still the nagging thought that the stolen mail could be hidden almost anywhere between the Anchorage post office and Merrill Field.

There seemed little reason to think the bush pilot who flew the small plane would take the mail to some cache deep in the wilderness; for one thing, landing might be a problem. So the investigation wore on, frustrated by many fruitless searches of the entire area.

Finally we decided to heed the tales of the trappers and traders of the north. We started to look for a converging of animal tracks in the snow. The trappers and traders say the fox is among the most curious of animals. After they cease to be afraid of a strange object in the snow, they can't keep away from it, going back periodically to investigate and anoint it.

Following the tracks of the wild animals in the snow finally led us to a central point where sacks of stolen mail, ripped open and gone through, had been discarded. The sacks had continued to be covered by the frequent snows of winter, but the animals had kept digging at it as they revisited the site to investigate.

It was clearly evident that the airline caretaker had been dumping mail from the truck after he rifled the sacks, going well off his usual route between the Anchorage post office and Merrill Field to do so. The caretaker was taken to the site and confronted with the huge pile of stolen mail. He later admitted his guilt.

If any explanation is needed to explain the curiosity of the fox and other wild animals, it is possible that the salty scent of perspiration adhering to the mailbags attracts them.

In 1945, I was assigned to make some long overdue audits of the small post offices in the Yukon River area that had been put aside during the war. The country was wild, expansive, beautiful, and unspoiled. The days were twenty-two hours long, and the weather was perfect. I saw the region before the roar of the bulldozers and the chatter of the pneumatic hammers split the peaceful solitude high above the slowly drifting water.

Starting out from Fairbanks by bus on the Steese Highway that ended at Circle, I hoped to pick up transportation as I went along. The first post office was at Miller House, where Postmaster Frank Miller and his Italian wife, Graziella, offered me food and lodging. For breakfast the next morning Graziella served ham and eggs and sourdough hotcakes. It was here that I learned that one- and two-year old eggs have a taste of their own that is foreign to the palate of the cheechako but preferred by the sourdough. I was able to hire a car to take me on to Central where Postmaster Riley Erickson, an old prospector, ran Central House.

After the audit at Central, I was lucky to catch a ride on a truck to Circle. Here the dirt road ended at the bank of the Yukon River. From now on, transportation would be by boat, or I would have to wait several days for a bush pilot to come along. During the audit the postmaster happened to mention that there was a Canadian boat in town that might take me downriver.

I went down to the waterfront and found the boat. It was a thirty-foot shallow draft riverboat that sported the name *Yukon Rose*. She was being taken from Whitehorse to Fairbanks to be used for freighting on the river by a man named MacKenzie and his partner. Captain Mac turned out to be a very friendly man who agreed to take me as far as Rampart, stopping at the post offices along the way long enough for me to make audits. He asked if a ten dollar fare would be too much, plus five dollars for a stateroom. The stateroom turned out to be a short bunk behind the wheelhouse. Meals were extra.

1945 picture of the old Central House on the Chatanika to Circle City dogsled mail route. Sourdough and Postmaster Riley Erickson stands at doorway.

Captain Mac said they would be leaving as soon as he stocked up. By stocking up, he meant buying a couple of quarts of whiskey at the store and a large salmon from the Indian who had a fish wheel nearby. The salmon was hung from the mast by its tail, and salmon steaks were henceforth cut from the head "upward" for each meal.

We got away at 10:15 A.M., and as soon as we reached midstream, the captain opened one of the quarts and announced that we would have to kill it before dinner because they needed the empty bottle to mash the potatoes. Between the captain, his partner, and a couple passengers, this feat was taken care of well before it was time to start dinner. Another ship's rule was that there would be no dishwashing. Everyone kept his own plate. If he was fussy, he could slosh it in the silty Yukon River water a few times.

After dinner I was lulled to sleep by a warm friendly sun, only to be awakened by a ten-year-old native girl who excitedly shouted, "Wake up, look at the Arctic Circle." I was a cheechako, but she wasn't fooling me—I knew you couldn't see the Arctic Circle. Not so; on shore someone had erected a large circular sign painted with the words ARCTIC CIRCLE.

Soon after six we arrived at Fort Yukon, one of the first Alaskan settlements on the river, and the following evening we were in Steven's Village. Here the postmaster had taken in several muskrat skins in payment for postage stamps. He claimed they were legal tender along the Yukon. How was I to know? And what is a muskrat skin worth—prime or otherwise? We settled the problem; I allowed him $1.50 per skin, and he agreed not to accept any more pelts for postage.

Steven's Village was a remote native trading village when I was there, isolated except by the river traffic in summer and bush planes in winter.

For decades Alaskans dreamed of a bridge across the mighty Yukon River. It was planned for Rampart—an apt name for the location of a suspension span—with the road to go on to Nome. But the black gold of Prudhoe Bay changed all that.

Long after I was there, a 24.5-million-dollar box-girder bridge

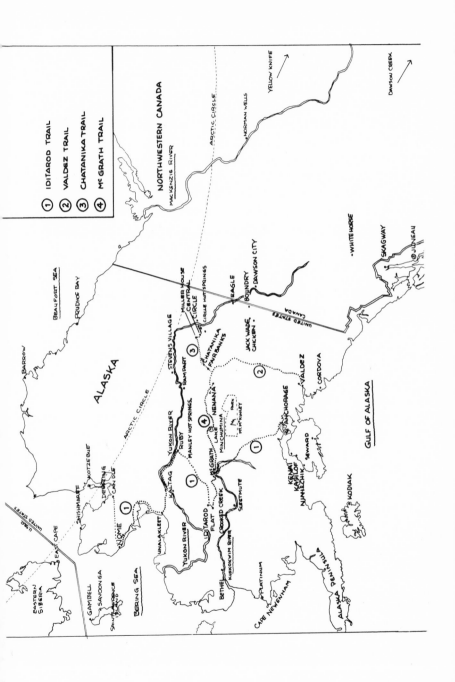

was built across the Yukon near Steven's Village. It was to carry the Alaskan oil pipeline and traffic on the Walter J. Hickel Highway north to the oil fields at Prudhoe Bay.

The next afternoon we arrived at Rampart. The *Yukon Rose* put me ashore. I walked the plank with a briefcase and a sleeping bag. I hated to see her leave. She was as rough as the country and had a crew to match, but a more hospitable craft won't be found anywhere today.

There wasn't much activity at Rampart. There was no place to sleep or to eat, and apparently there was no easy way to get out of town. Postmaster Clement Anderson, who was over seventy, ran the post office out of a corner in his one-room prospector shack. The old fellow had developed cataracts and couldn't read. How did he distribute mail? He just shuffled through the letters on hand until a watching patron stopped him by claiming a letter, which he handed over. He had several on hand that he had been shuffling for a couple of years with no takers. He said he didn't want anyone to come back to Rampart and not have any mail.

After the audit, the problem of moving on was brought up. The postmaster had an old wall crank telephone. He said it hadn't been used for several months, but if we were lucky we might raise someone at Manley Hot Springs, several miles south. After a lot of cranking, waiting, and cranking, someone in Manley did answer. Could they try to get a bush pilot to come up to Rampart to pick me up? They would "see," and then "ring us up." It wasn't too long before bush pilot Lon Brennan, who lived at Manley Hot Springs at the time, did call and say he would fly up after dinner.

Having a few hours to kill, I wandered around town and along the riverbank. I stumbled across an ivory Mastadon tusk partially hidden in the mud and grass. The local trader showed me his natural deep freeze. It was an old mine tunnel into the hill which penetrated about thirty feet into the permafrost. He bought salmon from the natives and kept them in his frozen mine until he had enough to hire a plane to fly them into Fairbanks.

True to his word, Lon Brennan came along and picked me up at the grass-covered, mosquito-infested landing strip. On the way back to Manley, he buzzed mountain sheep grazing on the green mountaintops.

A good dinner at Manley, a bath in the hot waters, and a good night's sleep in a real bed were welcome. The next day I flew back to Fairbanks and civilization with its many rules, laws, and regulations. The delightful informality of the people and the majestic beauty of the country were deeply missed. In the days to come, if you drive across the bridge on the Yukon, you might miss the atmosphere of the 1940s, but the area will still be as immense, spectacular, beautiful, and quiet. Well, almost as quiet.

3

The Black Bear Case

HUNDREDS OF commemorative stamps have been issued. They have honored the pony express, the stagecoach, the iron horse, and the airplane; but not one was ever printed to honor the Alaskan malamute or the mushers who drove the mail-sled dogs in the north before other means of communication existed.

The Alaskan malamute was the work dog of the north. They were the dogs who could take the punishment of pulling their own weight and more over a trail of ice and snow in below-zero weather on thousand-mile trips each month.

The hardworking mushers who carried the mails winter after winter, like most workingmen, have found history to be silent about their exploits, no matter how heroic they may have been.

If it hadn't been for the willing malamute, capable of performing in the severe weather the Arctic offers, the isolated and scattered mining camps and small villages spread over three hundred thousand square miles of the northern part of Alaska would have had no communication with the outside world and no mail, medicine, or supplies from freeze up in October until break up in April or May.

Throughout the history of mankind, dogs have been bred for a great variety of useful purposes. Three breeds are normally thought of as sled dogs: the Alaskan malamute, the Siberian husky and the Samoyed. Almost any kind of dog that was large enough was used as a sled dog at one time or another. There was little care or thought in the breeding of sled dogs in the early days; each musher used what he had or could get.

When the explorers, prospectors, traders, and missionaries first came north, they found that the Eskimo was using the malamute as a work dog. Explorer-missionary Hudson Stuck wrote that the same dog was found from Greenland to Nome and was assumed to be a descendant of the arctic wolf. From 1906 until 1917, Nome, Alaska, was known as the place to come if you wanted the best sled dog available. Arctic explorers Roald Amundsen and Vilhjalmur Steffansson came to Nome for their sled dogs. Dogs selected for one of Admiral Peary's arctic explorations were turned over to Leonhard Seppala in Nome when that particular venture of Peary's was canceled.

The malamute is fully acclimated to the north, weighs around a hundred pounds, and can pull more than his weight in freight and mail all day long, loving every minute of it. He has dense fur, tough feet, short legs, pricked ears, a bushy tail, a silver-gray muzzle, slanting eyes, and a black nose. The Alaskan malamute, although affectionate and faithful, was a working dog in the early days and not treated as a pet. Even today, the American Kennel Club lists the malamute under the category "working group." The North American weight-pulling record was held by an Alaskan malamute.

Until the 1970s, the malamute was rare in dog shows, but he is now winning firsts and even some bests in show awards. This dog has been found to make an excellent pet and companion despite his formidable appearance and great strength. Malamutes are light eaters for their size, hardy, keep themselves clean, and are strikingly beautiful animals. Clifford Price, now of Freeland, Washington, was chief clerk in the Army Quartermaster Corps at Fairbanks, Alaska, during the war years of the early 1940s. He remembers the K-9 Corps was breeding Alaskan wolves with malamutes for working sled dogs at that time. He was told by the K-9 Corps personnel that if the young wolf-malamute pups lapped milk from a dish, they were kept; but if they sucked at it, they were eliminated as being too wild for domestication. It is possible some of these K-9 bred Alaskan malamutes are the forebears of today's big powerful champion malamutes.

Another working dog, the Samoyed, is white. This dog was used as a draft animal as long ago as 1893 on an expedition by Norwegian Fridtjof Nansen in his unsuccessful attempt to reach the North Pole.

The Siberian husky was brought to Nome by Fox Maule Ramsey, a mining man, around 1910 from the Kalima River area of Siberia. The Siberians are lighter dogs than the malamutes, weighing from forty-five to sixty pounds, and their tails curl up over the back. They are said to be more gentle than the Alaskan malamute.

Over the years it became usual for most people to call any sled dog a husky, whatever the breed or mix. In fact, there were those who contended that the husky was a breed of its own—long and rangy with longer legs than the malamute, with ears not as permanently pricked up—and no relation to the Siberian husky. Mike Shepard, a former postmaster at Anchorage, remembers that dog teams at most of the roadhouses along the old Valdez Trail in the 1920s and 1930s had a similarity in color and markings that indicated good breeding. One thing is certain: the Alaskan malamute of today is a product of evolution and not a man-made breed.

There are some who contend that the true Eskimo sled dog is not the malamute but a dog called *kingmik* by the Eskimo. It is very likely the early-day explorers who picked their dog teams in Nome and throughout the north were not true connoisseurs of dog breeds. They were looking for dogs that could do the job, and their ancestry was merely incidental.

The true Eskimo dog is purported to have been brought to the Arctic by the Thule migration of Eskimo about two thousand years ago. There is the probability that the malamute could have been a descendant of the kingmik dog, and/or wolf, long before the whites came north looking for work dogs.

The two breeds are quite similar. Both are sixty-five-to eighty-five-pound dogs with heavy coats and furred feet that will not become hurt or cut during long periods of pulling a heavy sled on the trail. Both the malamute and the kingmik are strong, heavy-chested, thick-necked dogs with powerful legs. Both can work day after day in extreme cold weather on very little to eat. The kingmik has a heavy mane and a bushy tail that curls up over the back. Both dogs surely qualify to be called dogs familiar with the north (*Canis familiaris borealis*).

William J. Carpenter of Yellowknife, Northwest Territories, Canada, will give anyone a strong argument in favor of the kingmik as the original sled dog of the Eskimo. He has devoted his life to saving the breed. So far the kingmik is not registered as a breed with either the American or Canadian kennel clubs, whereas the malamute is.

Sled-dog trainer Leonhard Seppala went to Alaska right after the Nome gold rush shortly after the turn of the century. He was one man who could afford to be selective in breeding sled dogs in the early days. Seppala has passed away, but it would be interesting if he and modern-day breeder William Carpenter of Yellowknife could compare views on the subject of sled-dog breeds.

Seppala had a fortunate working relationship with the Nome mining company that employed him. They paid to feed his kennel of about thirty dogs in exchange for their hauling during the winters. In 1915 it cost about one hundred dollars a year to feed a sled dog properly, and with a kennel of thirty, Leonhard could not have otherwise met a three thousand-dollar annual feed bill himself.

Information on racing sled dogs is much more accessible than on working sled dogs. Dog races even in the early days of this century made news, and stories of the racing dogs are common. Scotty Allen, who won the first All-American Sweepstakes in 1908, used a crossbreed of malamute and bird dog. This was a 408-mile race from Nome to Candle and back. However, most of the big dogs, such as the Labrador and St. Bernard, were found unsatisfactory even when bred with the malamute because their feet would not stand up on the trail.

Seppala was a neighbor of ours in Seattle in 1953 after he retired and left Alaska. He had envied Scotty Allen, John Johnson, and John Hegness, who had all won the famous All-Alaska Sweepstakes. He noted that John Johnson, who started using Siberian huskies, was able to beat Scotty Allen and win the sweepstakes. Johnson's favorite lead dog was Kolma, a black Siberian with white eyes. Seppala began to breed the little Siberians for racing. He selected his lead dogs with a great deal of care, considering their trail sense, obedience, leadership, and intelligence. He always had a close relationship with his lead dogs because their very lives often depended upon one another. His favorite was a small Siberian he named Togo, a born leader. Finally, in 1915, and again in 1916 and in 1917, Seppala won the All-Alaska Sweepstakes with his Siberians, along with other tough races. With lighter loads than those carried by the mail and freight carriers, the Siberian was faster than the malamute. Another of Leonhard's lead dogs was named Balto. Balto was not particularly favored by Leonhard, but he was the lead dog who made the final relay that took the serum to Nome in the 1925 epidemic. In memory of the event, a bronze statue of the malamute Balto was cast and placed in New York's Central Park. Leonhard always felt that the statue should have been of Togo, who carried the serum the greatest distance, gave his all in the effort, and had to be retired after the ordeal.

Now, every March, forty or more dogsled drivers with their teams and favorite lead dogs gather in Anchorage to compete in the longest, toughest annual running of any race in the world. Called the Iditerod Trail Championship, the race was instituted in 1973 by Joe Redington of Knik, Alaska, as a grand nostalgic return to old-time dogsled racing. For endurance, the closest thing to the Iditerod was the All-American Sweepstakes. Of course, there are many dogsled races in Alaska today, but most are over much shorter courses.

The Iditerod Trail Championship race follows the old trail that brought mail and supplies to such mining camps as Flat and Iditerod. It is a most severe test of both man and dog. No purse could adequately pay for the hardships encountered over the route. Still, there are many who enter to enjoy the competition, never really expecting to win. It requires a great deal of teamwork between man and dog, and a truly husky dog to survive the route.

The Iditerod Trail, the Valdez Trail, and many others were traveled day in and day out in the early days in Alaska by tough dog team mushers and dependable sled dogs. The pioneer dog mushers of Alaska were as hardy a breed of man as you could find on any frontier. They were the ones who really opened up interior and northern Alaska, giving faithful service for well over a quarter of a century before any attempt was made to carry mail and supplies by air.

Gold strikes at Fairbanks, Nome, and later at Flat and Iditerod attracted a horde of prospectors, traders, fortune hunters, and others. All these people expected mail service and had to have supplies. Seattle was their port of embarkation, and before the Alaska Railroad was finished in 1923, ships unloaded at the ice-free

Photo of a changing time, from the sled dog to the bush plane (Fairbanks, Alaska, 1930). Bennett-Rodebaugh, after two changes, was bought by Pan-American when they started flying into Fairbanks. Left to right, A. A. Bennett (pilot), Ed Young (pilot), Charlie Thompson, Genevieve Parker, Tommy Girard (part owner), Leonhard Seppala (dog-team racer), sled driver unidentified, Sigurd Seppala in sled.

port of Valdez. From there mail for the interior went five hundred miles over the Valdez Trail to Nenana. Then the routes fanned out to serve a vast northland.

To haul the mail, people, and freight, working sled dogs were developed around the Eskimo's malamute. There is a report of one effort to use reindeer to draw a mail sled, as was done in Lapland. The reindeer as a mover of freight and mail never worked out in Alaska. They were not readily available, and much of the terrain over which mail was moved was not suited to this mode of transportation.

Horses were brought north with the stampeders of 1898, but the winters were too severe most of the time to make the use of the horse practicable. So it fell to the lot of the working dog to provide the essential part of the mail transportation system during the winters. In the summer, the sternwheeler and other shallow draft riverboats were used. This was the way mail and freight were moved in the north until well into the 1930s.

It was not unusual for a mail carrier to travel four thousand miles during a winter, carrying loads of well over one hundred pounds for each dog in his team. Thirty miles a day was an average run, with relay stations every 100 to 150 miles. Drivers would meet at the stations, exchange mail, then return to their home station.

On the mail routes, the most frequent service was weekly, but few of the routes operated that often. Mail contracts were bid on, and in 1925 the Northern Commercial Company had the mail contract from Fairbanks to Unalakleet, the longest in Alaska. A load limit of eight hundred pounds was set, and occasionally when this was exceeded, two sleds were hooked together tandem.

Explorer and missionary Hudson Stuck traveled in Alaska and the Canadian Arctic extensively in the early days. He had this to say about the U.S. mail carriers: "So far as there is anything heroic about the Alaskan Trail, the mail carriers are the real heroes. They must start out in all weathers, at all temperatures, they have a certain specified time in which to make their trips, and they must keep within that time or there is trouble. The bordering country of the Canadian Yukon has a more humane government than ours.

There, neither mail carrier nor anyone else, save in some life or death emergency with license from the Northwest Mounted Police, may take horse or dog to start a journey when the temperature is lower than forty-five degrees below zero. But I have seen a reluctant mail carrier chased out at sixty below zero, on pain of losing his job, on the American side.''

For we cheechakos who didn't reach the Territory of Alaska until the early 1940s, there were few of the dogsled routes left. I happened to be in Nenana on November 3, 1945, when one of the last remaining dogsled mail routes came into town from Lake Minchumina, a hundred or so miles west. The driver first stopped at the post office, where he delivered a mere handful of letters and then asked the postmaster for his pay. Only he and a few others remained at Lake Minchumina during the winter, and that post office had been discontinued. Here was a man who was making a two hundred-mile dogsled trip once a month to carry his own mail. He did have a beautiful team of dogs, but it was only a short time until the Post Office Department tired of this "subsidy" and abolished this dogsled mail route. The last dogsled mail route, Savoonga to Gamble on St. Lawrence Island in the Bering Sea near the International Date Line, was not displaced by the airplane until 1952; but those in the Alaska interior had been displaced many years prior to that.

Walter Jewell and Maurice O'Leary had the mail contract between Chatanika and Circle City for years. During the summers they drove a buckboard over the road, and during the winter they used a horse-drawn sled, falling back on their dog team only when the weather became so bad the horses couldn't be used.

Out of the twenty dog mushers who relayed the serum over the mail trail from Nenana to Nome in 1925 during the diptheria epidemic, only two were regular mail carriers. One was Bill Shannon of Nenana, who made the first relay, and the other was Fred Milligan, who later carried mail from Nenana to Lake Minchumina in the 1930s. Fred kept watching the bush plane replace the dogsled routes. He finally realized he couldn't beat them, so he joined them. He quit sledding, moved to Fairbanks, and went to work for Pan-American Airways when they first came into Alaska.

Driving a dog team almost always during below-zero weather was work. The dogsled races, however, although just as rigorous, were fun. They appealed to the sourdough's thirst to gamble. So it was the dog mushers and the lead dogs who entered and won the sled-dog races who usually gained recognition.

There was one mail-sled musher who did gain recognition of sorts. He was William F. Duffy, who carried the mail in the Iditerod gold field area. Through no particular fault of his own, he happened to be the musher when a registered mail pouch containing over thirty-two thousand dollars in currency disappeared from his sled one night when he stopped over at a roadhouse operated by one William Schirmeyer.

In those days it was the custom in Alaska to leave a loaded sled outside overnight. Mail was hallowed by Eskimo and sourdough alike, and thefts were unheard of.

The case was soon to be known as the Black Bear Case, after the most colorful character among several suspects. This character was Nellie Beattie, a prostitute who had a house on the line at Flat, Alaska. Nellie was well known from the Klondike to the Iditerod as the Black Bear. This trademark adhered because her body was covered in places with a dense growth of black hair.

The Black Bear, a large attractive woman of forty, had been in the north for twenty years following the Klondike Stampede of 1898. She had remained at Flat after the Iditerod Stampede and had acquired property reported to be worth about thirty thousand dollars. She had a reputation of being shrewd, intelligent, and unscrupulous, according to Star T. Pinkham, the post office inspector who investigated the case for the Post Office Department.

It was not unusual for a miner to owe a prostitute as much as eight hundred dollars for services performed during the long winter when he couldn't get out on the creeks to work his claim. In addition, the Black Bear would loan money at high interest rates to good-risk miners who might need it to carry them through a winter.

The case wasn't an easy one to investigate. The theft had occurred in the dead of night in a very remote northern land where intense storms were frequent and daylight barely lasted five hours. Inspector Pinkham, an attorney, was a capable, highly respected investigator who lived in Seattle. The currency disappeared the night of December 30, 1922, and the inspector had to travel by steamship to Seward, by rail to Nenana, then by dogsled to Iditerod. Consequently, he wasn't able to reach the scene of the crime until February 11, 1923, forty-two days after it happened. In those days there were no post office inspectors living in Alaska, and any mode of travel was slow and infrequent, particularly dogsled travel. He was joined in Iditerod by E. G. Wetzler of Nenana, who was chief clerk of the Railway Mail Service in Alaska and had charge of all transportation of mail.

The first law officer to investigate was Deputy Marshal Lynn Smith of Iditerod. Even Marshal Smith couldn't begin his investigation until January 11, when he interviewed musher Duffy at Flat, Alaska. Marshal Smith then set out by dogsled and made his investigation at all points along the trail.

Registered mail in those days required a person-to-person receipt, and each post office along any mail-sled route was required to sign a way bill for registered pouches carried on the routes. The lost pouch should have been easy to trace, but it wasn't. The entire pouch, containing a bundle of registered letters, was lost. The particular item of consequence in the case was register 104986, containing thirty thousand dollars, mailed by the Dexter Horton Bank at Seattle to Thomas P. Aitkin, McGrath, Alaska.

Fate marked the consignment for disaster and paved the way for temptation. The letter was mailed October 10, 1922, and as Inspector Pinkham wrote to the United States attorney in Fairbanks, "It suffered more vicissitudes of fortune and has been subjected to more irregularities in handling than probably any article of mail matter heretofore entrusted to the Postal Service."

The currency in the article was of general circulation and not distinguished by being new or bearing numbers in any sequence.

The currency packet arrived at Nenana on October 21, where it was placed in a mail pouch with sixty-eight other registered letters, and the pouch was addressed to McGrath. The pouch was inadvertently locked with a special lock used only on register pouches. This was the first link in a chain of events that contributed to the theft of the pouch, because the only post office on the trail that had a key to open it was the one in Flat. McGrath, where the pouch was to go, had no register-lock key. The mail didn't go out from Nenana immediately but was held fourteen days before the first winter dispatch by dogsled departed.

It was 250 miles to McGrath over a new trail that was not well marked and was occasionally broken by open water, for it was early in the sledding season. The mail was carried in a large basket type of sled capable of handling twenty-one hundred pounds of mail. The dog teams that pulled this weight normally averaged twenty-one dogs.

Different mushers were assigned to each relay. On the second relay, musher Charles Armour lost the trail and was unable to find it for days. In the meantime, he cached the mail in the woods. When he did find the trail and reloaded the mail, he was twenty days late and had been lapped by two subsequently departing mail-dog teams.

When the register pouch arrived at McGrath, the postmaster thought it was for some other office because she had no key to open it. She sent it out with musher William F. Duffy, asking him to inquire of the postmasters along the line if they had a key that would open it. She could have slit and opened the pouch to learn if the mail was actually for McGrath, but to do so would have precipitated a great deal of bureaucratic correspondence. But she had already received inquiry by telegraph about the delay in delivery of the thirty thousand-dollar currency-register shipment.

Six days later, musher Duffy arrived at Flat, the end of his route. He delivered all the mail to Ralph Rivers, a young man who was later to become an attorney and Alaska's first congressman when the territory became a state. Ralph Rivers was working in the Flat Post Office, assisting his mother, who was the postmaster.

Duffy told Rivers that there were some missing registers at McGrath, one of which contained thirty thousand dollars. Duffy stood by while Rivers dumped the contents of the register pouch on the floor, then stooped down to examine the various articles. He then told Rivers, "I think this is it. I'll send a wire to the McGrath postmaster."

Rivers put all the mail back into the pouch, addressed it to McGrath, and locked it with an iron lock that could be opened by the McGrath postmaster.

Duffy then departed to visit the girls on the line. There he made arrangements to take two of them along on his return trip. Nellie Beattie, the Black Bear, wanted to go to Seattle, and another of the girls, Nadine Saum, wanted to go as far as Iditerod. This would be possible because the return mail would only amount to seventy-seven pounds, compared to the approximate twenty-one hundred pounds the sled was capable of hauling. Incoming mail—with papers, magazines, and many parcels—was considerably heavier than outgoing mail.

Duffy didn't get away on the return trip until 3:00 P.M. the next day. They left with Duffy at the gee pole of the sled, Nellie riding at the handlebars, and Nadine as passenger in the basket with the outgoing mail. Their load included a sack of sausage, dog food, and all the baggage of the two girls. As Duffy left, three other dog teams fell in behind, each with one or two of the girls from the line. They all planned to throw a farewell party for Nellie, the Black Bear, at Schirmeyer's roadhouse, the next stop beyond Iditerod.

When he stopped overnight at Iditerod, Duffy took the register pouch to the bank, where he left it for safekeeping. On the way he stopped by the pool hall, with the pouch thrown over his shoulder, to chat. It was presumed by this time that almost everyone within a wide area knew there was a thirty thousand-dollar currency shipment in the pouch, for the Alaskan Mukluk Telegraph (grapevine) in those days was incredibly active and efficient.

The next day, Duffy loaded the mail on the sled before anything else, so that the register pouch would be on the bottom of the load and not apt to fall out of the basket-shaped sled. The mail was covered with what little freight he had, and then the Black Bear loaded her considerable belongings. A tarpaulin was lashed over the load. It was only a short distance of sixteen miles from Iditerod to Schirmeyer's, where they arrived early. The Black Bear unloaded the possessions she would need overnight while Duffy unhooked and fed the dogs.

At Schirmeyer's the drinking started almost as soon as they arrived. They were joined by Sig Wiig and his passenger, Virginia Howard, as well as by musher Chester Brink and others. The only two who didn't drink were the Black Bear and Schirmeyer. The party broke up about midnight, and all found bunks; Duffy slept with the Black Bear.

The next morning Duffy awoke with a hangover and went out early to ready his dogs. Chester Brink, who was outside, said to him, "I threw your stuff back on the sled."

Duffy later said he thought some of the dogs had been trying to get at the sack of sausage that was on the sled and gave no thought to checking to be sure the mail was still on the sled. After the Black Bear had loaded her baggage, he lashed down the tarpaulin and they left. Duffy didn't look to see if the register pouch was on the sled until two days later when they reached Ophir. At Ophir he discovered the register pouch was missing.

At this point, Sig Wiig, who was traveling along with them with his passenger, Virginia Howard, offered to retrace and search for the pouch if Duffy would furnish dog food, but Duffy declined. Strangely, the postmaster at Ophir signed the way bill, acknowledging that she had checked the register pouch through her post office. The next stop was at Takotna, where the postmaster also signed the way bill.

Upon their arrival at McGrath the loss had to be reported. The Black Bear went on her way to Seattle. It wasn't until January 7 that Deputy U.S. Marshal Lynn Smith of Iditerod received word of the loss. He interviewed Duffy, and by the eleventh he set out on his investigation, stopping at all post offices and roadhouses on the mail route from Iditerod to Takotna. Marshal Smith learned that Duffy had told the Iditerod postmaster that he "had that sack, and there is no record of it, and it would be easy to get away with it."

Inspector Pinkham and Chief Clerk Wetzler went over the same ground. They made a search of Schirmeyer's roadhouse and barn and talked to him at length. He seemed to be a harmless old man trying to make a living selling moonshine and food to what few travelers dropped by. They were reaching the opinion that Duffy had somehow conspired with the Black Bear to steal the currency and take it with her to Seattle. They talked to the Black Bear in Seattle when they returned from the north, but of course she denied being implicated in any theft. There really wasn't any evidence against anyone, only suspicion on the grounds of opportunity. Duffy and the Black Bear certainly had every opportunity to steal the pouch, and Duffy's actions on that trip didn't help his plea of innocence. The case seemed to be hopeless.

Then came the break. Three years later, Inspector Pinkham read a newspaper article relating how William Schirmeyer had lost a one thousand-dollar diamond ring while in a Eugene, Oregon, hospital. He was portrayed as an Alaskan prospector who had worked his fingers to the bone digging for gold in the frozen north only to be tricked by a sly nurse.

Inspector Pinkham knew Schirmeyer had never been a prospector or a miner. Schirmeyer was in Los Angeles, apparently living well beyond his means. Pinkham went to Los Angeles to talk to Schirmeyer again. Schirmeyer seemed glad to talk and to be the center of attention. He finally told Inspector Pinkham the whole story.

The night of the farewell party at his roadhouse, the Black Bear had suggested to him that they steal the register pouch from Duffy's sled. While all the others were drinking moonshine—most of which had been supplied by the Black Bear—she went out to the sled while Schirmeyer acted as a lookout. She got the pouch, and Schirmeyer hid it under the sawdust in his icehouse. They agreed to split the loot when the Black Bear returned the following spring.

Schirmeyer waited until the investigation had died down. Then he opened the pouch, again hid the registered letters that contained the money, and burned the pouch. He disposed of all the metal fittings after it was burned.

On her return north, the Black Bear stopped off at Schirmeyer's for a few days. They dug the registered letters out of the sawdust. The money had gotten damp, so the Black Bear ironed each bill to dry it out and smooth out the wrinkles. She and Schirmeyer split the loot, and the Black Bear went back to Flat.

Three years later Schirmeyer decided to go south and enjoy his fortune. He packed the money in a flashlight case.

In those days, and for many years afterward, it was extremely difficult to convict any sourdough of a nonviolent crime. The Black Bear was no exception. Even with her accomplice testifying against her, the jury could not agree on a verdict. The judge dismissed the jury and set a date for a new trial the next year. Schirmeyer pled guilty and was sentenced to a year in prison.

The second trial was held in 1927, almost five years after the theft. This time the jury found the Black Bear not guilty. Two years later the Black Bear married her old friend William Duffy.

Sig Wiig, the musher who had driven along with Duffy from Flat to McGrath and one of those who had been at the Black Bear's farewell party the fateful night the register pouch was stolen, lived in Ruby, Alaska. I was in Ruby in February 1946, and while I was there Sig asked me over to his house one evening to play a little poker. I suppose it was natural that the Black Bear Case would come up in the conversation. It was a case the sourdoughs loved to talk about.

Sig Wiig told me that he was subpoenaed as a witness at the 1927 trial of the Black Bear. Sig hitched up his dogs and mushed the three hundred or so miles from Ruby to Fairbanks in answer to the subpoena. He complained that he never could get the Department of Justice to pay mileage and per diem for his dogs on that trip. All they had paid him was the equivalent cost of an airplane ticket from Ruby to Fairbanks and return. Sig contended that traveling with his trusted dogs was a great deal safer than climbing into one of those 1927 flying contraptions. Sig had no better luck getting food for his dogs from the government than he had getting dog food from Duffy when he had offered to go back over the trail and look for the allegedly lost register pouch. There were those in Sig's house that night who felt that Duffy was in on the register pouch heist all along but that he had to marry the Black Bear to get his share of the loot.

Changes in the affairs of men are inevitable. The Pony Express lasted but a few months; the dogsled mail routes lasted over three decades. Better methods of communication and transportation spelled the end for both.

As in many things, those close to the romance often fail to appreciate it. Chief Clerk Wetzler who assisted Inspector Pinkham in the investigation of the Black Bear Case somehow missed the heroics of the faithful sled dogs and the work of the mushers. His job was to supervise the many dogsled routes in the interior of Alaska, and in the summer he supervised the mail boats and buckboard routes.

After one hard winter, Wetzler climbed aboard one of the Mississippi-type sternwheelers that plied the Yukon River in the early days. The captain of the vessel asked him how he had spent the winter. Wetzler replied, "I spent the whole winter doing nothing but looking at the ass end of a bunch of damn sled dogs. I'll be happy if I never see a dog again."

It's sometimes hard to please everyone. For the most part, those mushers had a deep respect for their dog teams and a close relationship with their lead dogs in particular. As rough as the work was, they must have enjoyed the life, or they would have returned to a world where the climate was more hospitable.

4

Plane Crashes, Train Wrecks, and Earthquakes

PROTECTING THE mail of the public became a very serious matter in the 1800s, when our country was in dire need of some thread to help bind it together. Vast areas had been purchased and acquired that were mostly unknown, and the people living in those areas knew little about the United States of America. Pioneers in the Wild West were often lonesome, and messages from home meant the difference between being able to tolerate the raw life and giving up and going home.

Following the discoveries of gold in Colorado Territory in 1858, a trading center called Denver began to grow, and the communication needs of the determined pioneers were served by the Overland Mail, which operated between Atchison on the Missouri through Denver and on to Placerville in California. There were fifty-one stage stations along the route. The Overland Mail had excellent fast stagecoaches that made the trip between Atchison and Denver in six days. The main line of the stage came into Denver down Larimer Street to Cherry Creek at Twelfth.

In those days the event of the week was the arrival of the stage. Everyone listened for the stage driver's bugle blast heralding the arrival of the four-horse hitch as it thundered down Larimer Street. The Overland from the East would have the mail, a few new faces, and perhaps a strongbox carrying money to pay for the gold that was pouring out of the mountains in the West.

There were no telegraph lines over which messages could be sent in 1860. The mail meant everything, both personally and commercially. This was a time when slogans like "The mail must go through" were reborn. Stage drivers were told repeatedly that nothing must ever stop the mail. Stage drivers lived up to the spirit of the slogans. When stages were held up by outlaws or ambushed by Indians, the drivers would rarely abandon the stage until the mail was hidden or they were rescued, even when passengers had been killed. It was a matter of pride to show that they could bring the mail through. Mail was an emotional thing, and those rough pioneers were never in a mood to condone abandonment of it, and stage drivers knew this. Such dedication was not limited to the Overland Mail, it was equally true on the Butterfield, Wells Fargo, and other stage lines.

Stagecoaches were fast for the times, but some wanted even faster service, so the pony express was born. The idea for a pony express may have come about because of the success of Charles Bent's pony express eighteen years earlier, which ran between Fort St. Vrain, Bent's Fort, and Taos along the foothills east of the Rocky Mountains. In January 1860, William Russell and Ben Fecklin of the Central Overland California & Pikes Peak Express contracted to provide a pony express from the Missouri to the Pacific. While a youngster of ten, Buffalo Bill Cody began his career as a pony express rider. Along the pony express route there were stations where the riders exchanged horses. Legend has it that on one occasion Buffalo Bill Cody rode 384 miles nonstop because no rider was available to relieve him along the way.

In their advertisements, Russell and Fecklin solicited "Young, skinny, wiry fellows, anxious for adventure and a chance to see our great West. Must be expert riders, willing to risk death daily. Orphans preferred. Sixty dollars per month and keep."

The famous pony express was a costly venture, and the five dollars charged for carrying a letter to California didn't pay for the service. The operation nearly broke Russell and Fecklin. Four years later, when the telegraph line had been strung across the West, there was no longer a need for the pony express.

Similarly, when the rails were joined in 1869, the need for cross-country stage lines was over, except through territory where railroads were not yet built, and the colorful stage lines were gradually replaced by the Iron Horse. The spirit of dedication to carrying and protecting the mail in the 1860s was branded into the culture of our country, and the depth of the brand remained an inspiration to those who handled the mail for almost a century.

It was the Overland Mail itself that really brought about the birth of what was to be called the Railway Mail Service. Mail from the East began piling up at St. Joseph, Missouri. Departing mail stages were either forced to wait for the mail to be sorted and placed in mailbags or, worse, they left without some of the mail. This caused a serious bottleneck, and action had to be taken to get the mail ready in time for departing mail stages. Separate mailbags were made up for the stages to throw off at places like Denver, Salt Lake City, Virginia City, and Placerville. William A. Davis was superintendent of mails at St. Joseph, Missouri, which was the main mail-distributing point for stagecoaches and the end of the line for the railroad from the East. On May 23, 1862, Davis placed in operation his scheme for getting the mail ready for the departing stages on time. He hired clerks to ride the train into St. Joseph and distribute the mail "over the rails" before it even reached St. Joseph. The first railroad to have such a "railway post office" was the Hannibal & St. Joseph. Davis's plan worked so well he was promoted to supervise all overland mail distribution.

It was one of those periods when conditions demanded change. The Post Office Department could see the merit in having mail distributed on trains and authorized George Armstrong, the assistant postmaster in Chicago, to test the theory. Armstrong had the mail sorted on trains going in both directions and was able in this way to have mail ready for any station along the line, no matter where it was picked up.

Before mail was worked on trains, any mail for a town had to be put in a mailbag. Armstrong's plan eliminated a great number of mailbags. By the year 1878 the system was so well established that the Railway Mail Service was an important part of the post office system, and trains that carried mail cars were called Railway Mail

Offices. People could post letters in the railway mail cars while the train stood in a station. For towns where the trains did not stop, pouches would be thrown off, and an ingenious catcher hook would pluck an outgoing leather pouch off a pole as the train sped by.

In 1869 there were 27,106 post offices in the country. As the arteries of steel spread, the number steadily increased, and by 1901 the number peaked at 76,945 post offices. Since then, the number had been decreasing. As late as 1919, at least 80 percent of all post offices were small, part-time, one-person, fourth-class post offices. Today the number of post offices is little more than thirty thousand.

The love of the people for trains grew and thrived after the first aversion and fear of the unknown steam locomotive passed. Trains hold a very special enchantment for many, and railroad buffs today ride every train and visit every railroad station they can. Hobos, bindle stiffs, and bums—yesteryear's hippies—rode the trains and lived in railroad "jungles."

When the great transcontinental lines were finished, traveling by train became fashionable and comfortable. In the 1830s, you could hear old men deplore the passing of the glorious day of the canalboat and stagecoach. They couldn't appreciate a romance with the sleek, noisy, smoky trains. If those who missed the canalboats could have lived into the 1960s, they would no doubt deplore with feeling the passing of such luxury trains as the 20th-Century Limited, the City of San Francisco, the Empire Builder, the North Coast Limited, the Santa Fe Super Chief, or the Panama Limited. Most of the great passenger trains ran east and west, but the Panama, a sleek limited that followed the Mississippi Valley, ran from Chicago to New Orleans.

A railroad buff named Chester Williams of Edmonds gave me a copy of a nostalgic article on that famous train. I do not know its origin, but it is a classic piece of writing.

> The Panama will never be replaced in the hearts of the thousands of people to whom it is a timepiece and an inspiration. It was news when the Panama was late, a lavishly equipped train that made that

thousand-mile run in less than twenty-four hours. It was the pride and joy of the valley just as the City of Natchez and the Robert E. Lee were a few years before when folks did their traveling by steamboat. The Panama's fame was so great that small boys were promised trips in its club car as a reward for good behavior.

The train left Chicago several hours after its sister, the Creole Limited, and hurried through the corn belt to Carbondale, where it grabbed its St. Louis sleepers just at dusk and headed for the South. It crept out over that long Ohio River bridge just as the evening mists arose from the gaunt Mississippi nearby, and as it rattled across the span the engineer would sit on the whistle cord to tell his passengers that they were in the South and aheadin' for New Orleans.

Folks in Cairo often used to delay supper until three long sonorous blasts told the little city that the famous train was crossing the Mason-Dixon line. It made a few stops but blew for the plantations as a signal to extinguish the lights, and as it streaked down Paducah way, folks knew it was time for a good-night toddy.

It roared into Memphis about midnight, caught its breath, and hurried away across Mississippi. The pant of the engine would be heard for miles in that flat country, and the scream of the whistle as the engineer cried for green lights and a clear track told the planters that it was time to be up and about the early-morning chores.

The firebox cast an eerie glow on the levees in the murky predawn of the valley, and the whistle sounded mournfully down the bayous. Those who heard it year after year accepted it as a part of plantation life, much as they accepted the cotton gin, the mules, and the mortgage. Jackson, Mississippi, went to work by its arrival, and south Mississippi towns knew it was time for a mid-morning cup of black coffee as it thundered through the villages. Soon after it crossed the Louisiana line it overtook the Creole Limited and beat it into New Orleans by fifteen minutes.

Its passing will mean that thousands of folks who have used the Panama Limited as a timepiece will now have to buy clocks.

Another luxury train, the Empire Builder, was a part of the heartbeat of the northern plains, pacing the lives of the early settlers. The Empire Builder followed the high line across the top of the nation from Chicago to St. Paul, across Minnesota, North Dakota, Montana, Idaho, and into Puget Sound on the Pacific. Going east, she pulled out of Seattle at three in the afternoon on her two-day scenic trip to Chicago, leaving most of the local work for her sister, the Western Star, which left six and a half hours later. She allowed her passengers little more than thirty minutes to view the grandeur of the shoreline as she ran north along Puget Sound. Then she turned east and addressed herself to the long climb into the spectacular Cascades. The diner was busy as she glided down the Cascade eastern slope and then struck out for Spokane to pick up her Portland sleepers. She crossed the Rockies at Glacier National Park and then settled down for her fastest run along the Missouri River valley. She crossed the Mississippi at St. Paul where she paused to change engines and crews before her final sprint into Chicago.

The North Coast Limited, the City of San Francisco, and the Santa Fe Super Chief each crossed the continent on their own routes, each one farther south of the other. You could take your pick, and any one of these fast comfortable trains was a luxurious, leisurely way to cross the country.

Big and powerful as they were, the trains were never without problems. There were derailments, snowslides, blockades, and collisions. One of the most serious insofar as mail was concerned was a main-line head-on collision between two of the largest mail trains in the Northwest. The Great Northern Railroad operated Trains 27 and 28, which carried mail for the Northwest, Alaska, and the Pacific rim countries. These trains were pulled by three large diesel engines, carried one railway mail car where clerks sorted letter mail, and from ten to twelve boxcars full of periodicals and parcel mail. The trains ran each day, 27 westbound and 28 eastbound. They met each other near Chinook, Montana.

On the fateful night of April 3, 1952, eastbound train 28 was on the siding to let westbound train 27 pass. The engineer on train 28 was letting the train "drift" through the siding so that he could pick up speed when 27 had passed and was in the clear. He had turned off his headlight as a signal to 27 that he was in the clear on the siding. Without realizing it, he let 28 drift back out onto the main line with 27 bearing down at better than ninety miles an hour (which was slow for some sections of that line in Montana). Railway mail clerks were busy sorting mail in their car, which was carried close behind the diesel engines. When it was realized what had happened, there was no way to avoid a head-on collision.

Some of the trainmen were able to jump off, others were killed at their stations. The three-unit diesels on both trains were demolished by the impact, and about ten carloads of mail were broken open and scattered along the right-of-way. The mail clerks in the cars were thrown about inside the cars, being cut and torn by the many steel pouch racks and other equipment built into the cars. Amazingly, none were killed. One clerk lost his leg, and three others had to be taken to the nearest hospital. One clerk, although badly shaken, remained with the mail to protect it for more than fourteen hours. He was not told to; he simply met his responsibility as stage drivers had done years before.

It is the job of the postal inspectors to protect and recover mail in situations like this. Postal Inspector Carl A. Hoyer and I had been working on a case at Hays, Montana, nearby. We were able to reach the wreck the afternoon of the day it occurred.

The postmaster at nearby Havre sent trucks to begin to pick up mail that had been scattered along the prairie. The wreck was on track that paralleled a busy highway, and vandals were quick to rummage through the broken parcel mail. The Montana National Guard sent a small detachment to help guard the mail. Although the main line of the railroad was cleared in a short time, it took several days to recover all the mail that was spread along a quarter-mile right-of-way on a breezy Montana prairie.

The need for trains to carry mail diminished as time went by. The Railway Mail Service reached its peak and was thriving in full bloom from 1890 until 1907. Mail contracts were a sort of subsidy that often paid most of the operating expenses for some passenger trains. Improvements in other means of transportation, better highways, and faster trucks and buses slowly eroded the rail passenger service. Later, airlines began to get subsidies that often staved off bankruptcy, and some were written to cover any loss a certificated airmail carrier might suffer within any given year.

By the 1930s towns were growing where there were no railroads, and rail passenger service began to fall off badly. If a mail contract on a certain line was canceled, the train was pulled off. Then in 1963 the Post Office Department decided it was time to make another major change in the basic way mail was to be transported.

It was decided to bring mail into huge mail-handling centers where it could be worked and sorted in stationary mechanized units, then hauled back by truck out to towns and cities for delivery. Each mail-handling center was given what was called a ZIP code. This was a deathblow for the Railway Mail Service and spelled final doom to the romantic era of the deluxe passenger trains. It also heralded the beginning of Amtrak.

But major changes came slowly. Many in the hierarchy of the bureaucratic Railway Mail Service strongly resisted taking mail distribution off the trains. They felt compelled to stand up for a mail transportation system that had worked well for at least a hundred years. They had a good point, but if the new ZIP code theory were to work, sorting mail on trains was not part of the plan.

It was anticipated that sorting machines could be developed that would scan the ZIP code on letters and automatically sort them. Such optical scanners turned out to be expensive, complicated, and subject to error. The American public could not be asked, the U.S. Postal Service thought, to use standard-size envelopes with a blocked-out section where the ZIP code could be written in. As a result, automatic sorting machines are not yet used to any extent in the United States. Japan has about eighty in operation.

The selling job on the district and sectional-center ZIP code method of moving mail was intense. The Post Office Department, always politically motivated, began to promise overnight delivery service. Some members of Congress were skeptical. Congressman Arnold Olsen of Montana, a ranking member of the House Post Office Committee at the time, visited several European countries and found that overnight mail service between cities was common there.

There was one big difference between Europe and Olsen's Montana. In Europe, distances were short and population heavy. In Montana, distances were great, and the state is sparsely settled. Apparently the congressman showed a great interest in just how the Post Office Department planned to provide overnight mail service throughout the western states without asking for a great deal of money to accomplish the feat.

Both Congressman Olsen and Postmaster General John A. Gronouski visited Butte, Montana, in the summer of 1965 to see what problems they had in the West. James J. Symbol, the Regional Director, and I joined them in Butte. Postmaster General Gronouski talked to several hundred at a luncheon about overnight mail service and improved mail service. P.M.G. Gronouski was a well-educated man with no postal experience prior to his appointment. He had to rely on judgment formed upon information furnished by persons in the department. His stand in Montana, like Custer's, was his last. Soon after Butte, P.M.G. Gronouski was appointed ambassador to Poland, and Lawrence F. O'Brien was named postmaster general.

When the drastic change in the way mail was to be moved and distributed was made, and the sectional-center ZIP code system adopted, there was no longer as great a need to sort mail on moving trains.

There were many officials who did not believe the new system would be any better or more economical than the old one. Those in the Postal Transportation Division felt that taking the distribution of mail off the trains was a threat to their empire, and they reacted as might be expected. When Railway Post Offices were discontinued, they replaced them with Highway Post Offices. A Highway Post Office, or HYPO, was merely a large motor van equipped so that mail could be worked while in transit along highways. This method of distributing mail didn't fit in with the sectional-center concept any better than the Railway Post Office did.

It was part of the work of postal inspectors to ride the mail cars and report on the operation and usefulness of the unit. These recommendations were advisory and were usually not followed by the Postal Transportation Division.

The situation reached a climax in the West after recommendations had been made for discontinuance of ten Railway Post Offices and no action was taken on any of them. Charles A. McIntyre of the Bureau of Transportation in Washington, D.C., came to Seattle to find out why there was such a great difference of opinion between postal inspectors and the Postal Transportation Division. A conference that lasted all day and well into the night was held in my office among those involved. The immediate result was the discontinuance of three Railway Post Offices and the eventual discontinuance of six more, which took care of nine of the ten the inspectors thought should be discontinued.

We wondered why we were not getting pressure from the railroads when an attempt was made to discontinue a Railway Post Office. It was a simple matter of economics. Even with the money received for carrying mail cars, the passenger trains of the day were losing money for the railroads. When a Railway Post Office was pulled off a train, the railroad had a good reason for discontinuing the passenger train. A great many were discontinued.

So Railway Post Offices gradually were eroded away, but it took eight years for them to die. On April 30, 1971, the Western Star (called the Williston & Seattle Railway Post Office) Train 28, rode out of Seattle into history. It left at 10:25 P.M., and the mail clerks distributed mail "over the rails" for the last time. The few Railway Post Offices that were still in operation throughout the country suffered the same fate on that day. The years of enchantment working mail on the trains was over. The clerks were assigned to post offices near their homes. Only one Railway Post Office was retained—the one between Washington, D.C., and New York City. This was ironical because the Railway Post Office that survived was in the heaviest-populated area in the country, where the sectional-center concept was supposedly at its most efficient.

Protection of mail while it was being hauled on trains offered a challenge to postal inspectors. John Streich of the St. Paul Division gained the reputation of being a sort of Sherlock Holmes of the moving post offices. In an effort to actually see who was stealing mail on a train, Streich once concealed himself in a coffin that was being shipped in the Railway Express section of the car that carried mail.

The inspector had to bore some small holes in the coffin so that he could see out and, I presume, breathe freely. His effort was rewarded when he did actually see a mail clerk steal some mail. It must surely have added to the tensions of the moment when the lid of the coffin slowly opened and a postal inspector rose up to intone that the people's mail must not be molested.

John Streich was a meticulous man and exhibited it in everything he did. His reports had not only a straight margin on the left of the typewritten page but also a straight margin on the right as well. When he cut kindling wood at home for the fireplace, he would always cut the pieces precisely the same length, and he piled them neatly in a basement corner.

Mailbags are locked with a flat iron lock that can be opened by a mail thief if he has a key. Before John Streich, there was no way to know if a lock had been opened and then closed again. He needed to know if a mailbag had been opened while it was being carried on a train. He invented a lock that looked identical to all other locks, but one of the rivets that held it together would turn a notch when the lock was opened. John could then tell if a mailbag had been surreptitiously opened while it was being hauled on a train, bus, or truck.

Unlike post offices, there were no observation galleries on railway mail cars, and John Streich had to be inventive if he was to protect mail he had no way of seeing.

He was confronted with a situation where mail was frequently on a train a thousand miles before it was scheduled to come off at some remote post office. Here is where Streich used what was called a "test letter." This was nothing more than a simple letter filled with marked money. The trick was to arrange that such a letter would be handled by the person who was suspected of taking mail. It was a situation where the inspector had to be doubly sure before anyone could be accused of taking mail. By meticulous perseverance, John Streich was always able to pick out and come up with the guilty man. It was this kind of work that kept him busy for years, won admiration of his fellow workers, and gained for him assignments on some of the toughest cases the Inspection Service ever had. It also eventually won him the promotion to inspector in charge of the St. Paul Division.

During the past century, mail has been transported in many different ways to match the times and conditions. It has gone by pony express, stagecoach, railroad, ship, horse, reindeer, dogsled, airplane, and truck.

As late as 1926 there was still a winter mail route between McCall and New Meadows, Idaho, that went by sled. To permit the horses to walk on top of the snow, snowshoes were sometimes fashioned for them. It was amazing how adept horses can become in using them.

By 1898, the West was no longer a wilderness, and Alaska had become the Last Frontier. Thousands of gold seekers were flooding the Territory of Alaska, and they needed mail service. A man named John Clum had founded the Tombstone, Arizona, *Epitaph* on May 1, 1880. By 1888, mining around Tombstone had faded and things were getting dull. Along about that time the *Epitaph*

Horse with snowshoes ready to pull mail sled on the McCall to New Meadows, Idaho, Star Route 70151. Taken in 1926.

carried a story about the visit of a post office inspector in the area. Clum apparently thought it would be more exciting to be a post office inspector than an editor. He sold out and was appointed the first post office inspector for Alaska in 1898.

Clum followed the route of the "Trail of '98" to Skagway, Dyea, Whitehorse, Dawson City, and finally to Eagle, Alaska, where he set up a post office. He then took the Stern-wheeler *Seattle No. 1* down the Yukon River on its maiden voyage, setting up post offices all the way to the mouth of the Yukon at St. Michael.

The first overland truck mail service over the Alaska Highway left the railhead at Dawson Creek, Canada, on September 23, 1943, and arrived at Whitehorse on September 26. It was operated by the U.S. Army Postal Service and served Canadians as well as the military troops in the area. A few months later the service was extended into Fairbanks. Today, large semis haul the mail all the way from Seattle to Fairbanks and Anchorage throughout the entire year.

Many different ways have been used to move the mail since the first pony express rider saddled up in 1860. Other changes are occurring too. As Leonard Sheets, who retired after years of yeoman service for the postal inspectors at Seattle, recently put it, "The post office has given me a beautiful letter carrier in miniskirts, whose arrival is a joy to behold and whose departure isn't bad either."

You just can't call your letter carrier a "mailman" anymore.

One dark snowy night early in February 1946, the Alaskan steamship *S. S. Yukon* ran aground in Johnson Bay near Pinnacle Rock, about twelve miles southbound out of Seward, Alaska. The Gulf of Alaska can be as rough as any body of water; even so, putting a large steamship bow first onto the beach can be a little hard to explain.

The first I knew of the disaster was when bush pilot Clarence Rhodes landed on the frozen Yukon River in front of Ruby, Alaska, and told me he had been asked to pick me up. Clarence Rhodes later was appointed regional director of the U. S. Fish and

Wildlife Service in Alaska. My boss wanted me to go to Seward and attempt to recover mail that was still aboard the *S. S. Yukon*. So I left Ruby, where it was a calm, clear thirty degrees below zero, foolishly thinking that the coast at Seward would have more hospitable weather.

On February 14, I joined Capt. George W. Stevens at Seward. Captain Stevens was a salvage master of the Army Transportation Corps. Under V-Admiral Allan R. McCann, he had been one of those who helped rescue thirty-three survivors from the submarine *Squalus*, which sank in 1939 in two hundred feet of water off Portsmouth, New Hampshire. The captain had a salvage crew ready, consisting of two deep-sea divers who were to salvage mail; Army CID Agent Albert Biskerski; FBI Agent Wright, and two experienced seamen named Thorwald A. Skulstad and Walter Clayton. He also had promise of an army power barge and an eighty-foot ship. My job was to recover mail; the army was interested in recovering bodies of any of the eleven soldiers and civilians who had lost their lives after the *S. S. Yukon* had gone aground.

The next day we were ready, but another gale was pounding the beach where the *S. S. Yukon* rested. Postal Inspector C. Harry Carlson had visited the wreck on a rescue ship that had been taking passengers off the beach the day after the *S. S. Yukon* had grounded. At that time the ship had broken in two and the stern had sunk. Carlson had located the mail in a forward hold but under several feet of water, and so the divers were needed to bring it up. Since the trip was southbound, there wasn't much mail aboard, but we had learned that there were a few pokes of gold in the mail that had been sent out by placer miners in interior Alaska.

During the five days we had to wait for the storm to abate, time was spent talking to crew members of the *S. S. Yukon* at Seward, longshoremen who had loaded the mail, passengers off the *S. S. Yukon*, and steamship officials.

It was learned that shortly after the ship had gone ashore, all passengers were ordered on deck and held in the main recreation lounge until rescue operations could be started. Sometime soon after this, members of the crew and steward staff, and others, ransacked the staterooms, slit open suitcases, and stole any items that might have some value. One elderly man had declined to go topside and remained in his stateroom. The door was broken open, and he was required to stand helplessly by while his luggage was ransacked and his money and rings taken. In reply to his indignant objections, the brigands simply told him everything aboard was salvage.

No information was developed that any mail had been stolen or rifled.

An oiler on the ship stole several pieces of jewelry, cameras, rings, and a woman's fur coat, which he wore when he was taken ashore on the line. After the rescue, he attempted to sell some of the items he had taken in Seward, Alaska. The fur coat was identified by the woman who lost it, and she had him arrested.

A professor of sociology at Rockford College pointed out that a catastrophe releases the criminal instinct of man, and the actions of the ship's personnel was a frightening example of what men may do when catastrophe strikes and no police protection or other authority exists.

On February 18, the second storm had abated and the salvage detail set forth on two ships to visit the site. The salvage detail of seven went ashore in a dory. The only remaining vestige of the *S. S. Yukon* was the forepeak of the vessel. Several mail sacks were found along the beach ripped at the seams by the action of the seawater against the rocky beach. The parcels and mail that had been inside had been reduced to pulp. The only evidence of what was once mail was mangled metal and wire. It was surprising how almost anything that would wear, dissolve, or part was actually eaten up by the power of the waves beating it against rock outcroppings. There wasn't even any evidence of the planking and timbers with which the *S.S. Yukon* was constructed.

Having satisfied itself, the salvage detail prepared to put back to the ship. Getting off the beach on an incoming tide and rising wind became a serious problem. With the expert seamen being in the minority, the boat capsized several times before it could get over the first breaker. Everyone was soaked in the thirty-six-degree water with a cold February night coming on. Few in that salvage detail knew anything about launching a dory in flat water, let alone into the sea that confronted us.

The power barge, obviously anticipating our predicament, came within sixty feet of shore and threw us a line, then backed off, dragging dory and men through the surf with all hands bailing for dear life.

When we were jerked aboard the power barge, we wondered if the operation was really worth the risk, but men have gone through much more for a few pokes of gold in Alaska. It was the people's mail, and we had to be sure.

Part of the work of postal inspectors is to recover and guard mail at the scene of plane wrecks. Over the years I have hurried to the scene of many such disasters. However, one of the best descriptions of just what happens in these cases was reported by the postal inspector in charge of the Denver Division in 1955.

About 7:45 P.M. on the evening of November 1, 1955, a Denver television station interrupted its program to announce that a UAL plane that had departed from Denver a few minutes before, bound for Portland, Oregon, had exploded in the air and crashed northeast of Longmont, Colorado.

Inspector in Charge Robert Dunbar immediately instructed Inspector Carl H. Pollack, who was in Greeley and the one nearest the tragedy, to proceed with all possible speed to the immediate scene of the crash. His first mission was to see that the mail was protected, and he was asked to get to the spot without regard for roadblocks or rendezvous points being set up. Three other inspectors were sent north from Denver to contact UAL officials on the highway near the wreck.

The inspector in charge, with another of his men, along with Postal Transportation Manager Jack Glidden, obtained a manifest of the mail on board the plane, then picked up some empty mail sacks and headed north toward the scene of the crash.

The inspector in charge wrote, "There is not a village for over one hundred miles along that lonely road across the rolling prairie;

71

traffic was light. A cold gusty wind was blowing from the snow-covered mountains, and the car's headlights intermittently picked up tumbleweeds drifting across the road."

This was not the first time Dunbar had made trips on such missions. Within the month, he had followed the same road on the way to Medicine Bow peak, near Laramie, Wyoming, where a plane carrying sixty-six persons had crashed head-on into the face of a vertical cliff dropping twelve hundred feet from a twelve thousand foot ridge. There hadn't been much mail left to recover on that occasion. What mail had not disintegrated in the crash or been destroyed by the explosion and fire was blown into inaccessible crevices or onto narrow sloping ledges of the cliff where only eagles could reach—eagles and the wind.

Dunbar explained it this way: "Standing shivering by the glacial lake at the base of the cliff we could see the wind pick up scraps of paper, which spiraled higher and higher in the cold clear air until they topped the ridge and took off sailing higher and faster to the west across Medicine Bow National Forest."

As the inspectors rolled north in the dark, there was little conversation. On cases like this, men don't feel like talking.

When they all assembled at the rendezvous point, they could see the reddish-yellow glow of twin fires some miles to the northeast across the fields. A pilot car led the way as they followed a dirt road, then drove along the edge of a plowed field until the car could go no farther.

Inspector in Charge Dunbar wrote, "A helicopter milled in from the south and zigzagged across the area, coming down low and dropping flares. The flares lit up a wide path of debris with fragments of the metal skin of the plane, seats, personal effects, and crumpled bodies. The copter went on north over the twin fires and then turned back south and disappeared in the darkness. The forms of men roping off the area around the fires were silhouetted by the flames, which continued to burn throughout the night, the porous earth into which the oil and gasoline had seeped serving as a wick to keep the fires going."

At the crash site, the rescue crew was well organized, and

responsibilities were already defined, for the inspectors had worked with the same officials on other, similar, occasions. The Colorado State Highway Patrol placed roadblocks around the area in which debris had fallen to keep the morbidly curious out of the area.

The inspectors did not see any mail in the debris, but in the pale moonlight they could follow the path of debris to the south. They formed a skirmish line with wide intervals between men and zigzagged across the field, picking up scattered pieces of mail.

A civilian defense car came by with the report that there was considerable mail at the point where the tail of the plane had come to rest, two miles farther south of the place where the body of the plane crashed.

When they came upon the tail of the plane, Dunbar described the situation and the action as follows: "The tail had been cleanly severed just ahead of the elevators. It rested upright, pointed directly towards the main crash site, on even keel, and had come to earth so gently that it had not furrowed the plowed ground. Several distinctive orange-colored mail sacks were recovered, all of them badly torn. Some letters, tied in bundles, were scattered around, but none badly damaged, except that the ends of some envelopes were cut or shredded as though they had been thrown or dragged at terrific speed across the ragged edges of the metal skin of the shattered plane. The mail recovered there showed no evidence of fire or of being subjected to intense heat."

Of course, all the mail had to be examined for possible evidence of what had caused the crash. Youths who had slipped by the patrols and patrolmen, knowing what the inspectors were doing, reported other areas where scattered mail had been seen along a mile-wide swath. As they searched with their flashlights, probing the reeds of the marshy land, wild ducks would burst into flight, and half-wild cattle, recently brought from summer mountain ranges, would bunch up and run, only to turn and sniff and blow until their curiosity was satisfied.

The search continued in a wider area where the meadows had been flooded and half frozen in places that would not bear the weight of man, until a five-mile area was screened for mail. Finally, the clouds obscured the moon and it was useless to hunt further with flashlights. The chilling wind—and wet feet—forced the inspectors to delay further search until morning. They returned to the rendezvous point and picked up what mail had been brought in by other officials. They had recovered only a little more than one hundred pounds of letters for their night's labor.

The following day a crane lifted the nose of the plane, and two hundred pounds of mail were recovered from the forward cargo pit. Then further search of the wind-blown prairie was made, covering an area eight and a half miles long and four miles in width.

From manifests it appeared that most of the mail aboard had at last been recovered. The letters were mostly in such good condition they were sent forward immediately.

Inspector in Charge Dunbar had vividly described just what postal inspectors do when an airplane carrying mail crashes.

When reports of the massive Alaskan earthquake on Good Friday, March 27, 1964, filtered throughout the world, worried friends and relatives of Alaskans all wanted word of their loved ones. Telephones, telegraphs, and other public communications were broken off. It was soon to be learned that nearly twenty-five hundred families were displaced or seriously affected; 122 were dead or missing in the quake and tidal waves that followed. Geologists later reported that well over twenty-five thousand square miles of land rose from three to eight feet.

In Seattle by 8 P.M. (PST) television programs were being interrupted to report the catastrophe. We at once realized that mail service was going to be extremely important to many worried people. We had to find out as quickly as possible what the postal damage was.

Postal Inspectors Kenneth E. Johnson and B. J. Sparks were stationed in Anchorage. Since we couldn't reach them by phone or telegraph, we had to find another way. Remembering that in 1958 a Postal Amateur Radio Network was formed, we decided to try to contact Anchorage by ham shortwave radio. Post Office Maintenance Mechanic Erwin E. McCafferty was a member of the network and operated Station W 7 VHY in Seattle. Postal Inspector E. J. Ingebright went over to see what McCafferty could do for us.

By 9:00 P.M. McCafferty had already picked up a weak signal from KL 7 ENT in Anchorage, calling W 7 AG of Suquamish, Washington. After McCafferty got them together; in the parlance of ham operators, he rode "piggyback" to Alaska with Horace Boe of W 7 AG, Suquamish.

How KL 7 ENT in Anchorage got on the air is a tribute to ham operators everywhere. With the temperature in the low twenties, no electricity, gas, heat, or water, Les Haye, of KL 7 CKQ, and Daniel Wright, of KL 7 ENT, went into action immediately after the quake. They rigged up a high-frequency transmitter in Wright's auto, operating mobile on a whip antenna. The two kept the car going with gas scrounged by Haye's son Jim and operated for several days. One of the local radio stations in Anchorage got back on the air, and Dan Wright could phone them to broadcast messages and inquiries.

Inspector Ingebright at McCafferty's W 7 VHY had him relay a message to Wright through Horace, asking if the two postal inspectors were all right and, if possible, to get some report on the postal situation. About 2:00 A.M., Anchorage time, a reply was received that all postal personnel were all right. There was varying damage to postal buildings, but security was being maintained, and steps were already being considered toward restoring mail service on an emergency basis.

By this time it was 4:00 A.M. in Seattle and 7:00 A.M. in Washington, D.C. We called the chief inspector in Washington, which enabled the Postal Service to answer a flood of inquiries from around the country about whether or not they could write to Alaska.

At the time of the quake, 5:36 P.M., the two Anchorage postal inspectors were still in their office in the federal building. The stout building survived the tilting and heaving, with light fixtures dangling by wires and the furniture jumbling. Across the street buildings had sunk twenty feet, and the entire front of the new J.C.

Penney building collapsed into the street. When the shaking subsided, the two inspectors set out for their homes.

They found Inspector Johnson's Turnagin Arm home teetering on the brink of a bluff formed when the land that had once extended almost five hundred yards to the shoreline sheared off, taking all other houses except one with it.

One of their neighbors had lost two small children, who fell into a crevice that immediately closed over them. They took Mrs. Johnson, who was standing outside when they arrived, along with them to the Sparks's home, which had escaped the damage. Having settled their families, the inspectors then visited all postal units in town.

At the Anchorage Airport the flight control tower was down and the field was closed. The post office airport annex building had suffered structural damage, but the central portion seemed safe enough. Inside, the place was a shambles.

The following morning, a Saturday, all postal employees voluntarily reported for work despite their many personal problems at home. After a conference, all hands turned to cleaning up the mess. A portable generator was obtained to provide a little light, and two bottled-gas heaters were found for much-needed heat.

The local radio station announced that mail would be picked up around town from street collection boxes wherever possible. This gave a surprised public a chance to write home, and the response was heavy. Many letters, and even notes, were dropped in mailboxes, many without stamps. As the collections came in, the mail was placed in mail pouches uncanceled and unworked.

The first outgoing mail left about 12:30 P.M. Saturday on a Pacific Northern Airlines plane (now Western Airlines) leaving from Elmerdorf AFB Field near Anchorage. Seattle sorted, canceled, and routed the mail and sent it on.

By Monday, incoming mail from the Lower 48 states was being delivered by letter carrier in the areas that were not closed off in Anchorage. By Tuesday, the downtown post office was opened, and displaced persons began calling at general delivery for their mail. This amazing restoration of a vital communication system

76

was due in no small part to the self-sacrifice and plain hard work on the part of all postal employees in the stricken areas.

Anchorage was a start. In the meantime, ham operators were attempting to contact some of the smaller towns and villages in the earthquake area that were cut off. Bob Ovink, Station W 7 HDA, an enthusiastic ham operator in Kirkland, Washington, was able to contact Kodiak, Alaska, and reported that no postal employees were injured. He was able to learn of the condition of the post office buildings and supplied information to the postal inspectors, which helped in restoring service there.

With things again running well in Anchorage, the inspectors were able to visit other cities. Inspector John H. Rohrer was sent to Alaska to assist the local inspectors who had been facing a gigantic problem alone.

When it was all over, Inspector Kenneth Johnson, who had suffered great personal loss, demonstrated his fine sense of humor under the trying circumstances when he penned a brief note: "Confucius say: One earthquake equals three civil defense drills."

5

Burglars I Have Known

RED HENDERSON WAS an accomplished, professional, and interesting burglar. He devoted most of his life to safe burglary when he wasn't locked up, but he was locked up a lot.

Red was a perfectionist. He used nitroglycerin, usually prepared an ounce at a time in some quiet hotel room where cool running water was available. He called it "juice."

It was true Red could open a safe so gently with the proper amount of juice that the door would not even bump against the wall when it swung open.

Red was once asked if he taught the younger burglars some of the expert tricks he had picked up over the many years he worked at his trade. Evidently there was a generation gap in the burglar field, because Red replied, "No! You can't teach these young punks anything—all they want to do is take a maul and pound on a safe all night until they break it open."

One of the stories told about Red concerned his purported blowing of the safe in the New Westminster, B.C., Canada, courthouse just prior to the trial of one of his associates.

When the court convened, the prosecutor produced a wrapped article that had contained a large maul which had been used to break open a safe. It had been found in the suspect's possession. When the evidence was opened in court, a small Boy Scout hatchet was found in the wrapping instead of a large maul. It would have been impossible to open any safe with a small hatchet, and the prosecutor, at a loss for words to explain what had happened, lost the case.

Red thought this was a big joke and bragged about it often, but he never made the mistake of admitting it was he who gently popped the evidence safe in the courthouse, removed a large maul from the evidence parcel, and substituted the Boy Scout hatchet. Red considered it one of his better capers and emotionally, if not financially, rewarding.

Red was a Canadian, but he liked to visit the United States. When a safe was blown in a professional manner in one of the northwestern states, Red was usually considered to be one of the principal suspects.

On one trip to the United States he, a partner, and a twenty-three-year-old heroin addict known as Pat Novis, traveled as far south as San Francisco. Along the way they cashed 113 Canadian postal money orders that had been burglarized from a north Vancouver, B.C. post office. Each one was cashed for its full one hundred-dollar value. The three had a real fun trip, staying at the best hotels and enjoying every luxury.

Attempts to extradite the three for this caper were time-consuming and frustrating. When the extradition proceedings seemed to be going well, one or all three would be arrested in Canada for some local offense. Pat Novis was in and out of jail frequently on narcotics charges. Pat had started using heroin when she was fifteen, and when she made the trip to San Francisco with Red and his partner she had a fifty-dollar-a-day habit. It took a real good burglar in those days to keep the girl supplied with junk. Finally, extradition attempts were given up when Red and his partner were sentenced in Canada to long prison terms on habitual criminal charges. Professional criminals said they received the "Big Bitch," a takeoff on *habitual*.

In the 1950s, Pat Novis knew most of the heavy burglars in western Canada and could probably tell which jobs each had pulled, if she would. We were sure she knew who participated in the March 1954 robbery of the Greenwood Branch of the Seattle First

National Bank when police officer Frank Hardy was killed and two other police officers were wounded. The Seattle police and FBI wanted very much to talk to her about this and might have done so.

Along about this time we arrested a Canadian named Lester Terrance Teague for cashing in Seattle postal money orders he had stolen in a burglary. Teague was very talkative, and one day he told Fred Lombard of our office that he had been in the British Columbia Penitentiary with a John Wasylenchuk, who told him he had taken two Canadian burglars, Cliff Dawley and Maurice Talbot, to Seattle, where they held up the Greenwood Branch of the Seattle First National Bank in March 1954.

Wasylenchuk told Teague they had worn eyeglasses with false noses and used heavy makeup as a disguise. He said Dawley started shooting too fast and should have fired only to scare the police officers.

Brock Adams, who was later a congressman and then secretary of transportation, was the United States attorney in Seattle at the time. His office and the FBI made every effort to extradite and prosecute Wasylenchuk, Dawley, and Talbot.

For his protection after he had formally given evidence against Wasylenchuk, Dawley, and Talbot, Teague was transferred from McNeil Island Penitentiary to Leavenworth. He outlived Wasylenchuk.

We wanted very much to talk to Pat Novis about Red Henderson and their trip to San Francisco. Merchants, motels, and hotels, including the St. Francis in San Francisco, where the money orders had been cashed by the trio were out a total of $11,300.

During the investigation, M/Sgt. Jack Purdy of the Royal Canadian Mounted Police and I visited Pat when she was in jail in Vancouver, British Columbia. We picked a poor day to talk to Pat. When we arrived the matron said, "Pat has been a bad girl and she is in the hole!"

This meant that Pat was in solitary confinement. She was brought up to the office to talk to us. As soon as she learned we wanted to talk about her trip to San Francisco with Red, she said, "I'd rather be in the hole than talk to you two."

Sgt. Purdy and I didn't think this was any great boost for our reputation as good conversationalists, and Pat went back to the hole.

When Pat was out of jail, we again tried to talk to her. This time she was much more sociable. She was a very conwise girl; although she did talk at length, she never did divulge anything that would in the least way implicate her or her confederates.

In another Canadian case we met the Duhamel boys. At the time they lived in Port Coquitlam, a small town near the U.S. border. They were known to have made trips into the United States to burglarize post offices and to steal U.S. postal money orders, along with the equipment for making them out. They would either cash the money orders or sell them to some fence. These boys did well until we happened upon one of the best stool pigeons I have ever known, a fellow named Brown.

Unlike most confidential informants, as they prefer to be called, who cooperate because the law has something on them, Brown worked for the sheer fun and excitement of it. He enjoyed police work so much he would have been in law enforcement, except for the fact that he had done time here and there and could never get cleared for anything but undercover work.

On behalf of the government, Brown made a few trips alone to Port Coquitlam in an effort to arrange to buy some of the stolen money orders from the Duhamels. Being fairly well acquainted with many professional criminals, he had little trouble gaining the confidence of the Duhamel gang, even to the point of learning a code the boys used in writing to each other, particularly when one of them was in prison somewhere. The code was in the punctuation. For instance, an oversized period at the end of a sentence had a meaning, a circle instead of a dot above an *i* had another meaning.

Finally one of the Duhamel boys agreed to sell Brown some money orders for five hundred dollars. During the fifties, five hundred dollars was not exactly petty cash, and we had some difficulty convincing the chief postal inspector that we should turn a stool pigeon loose with this amount of money in a foreign country.

When we finally had approval and had exchanged the five

hundred dollars for Canadian currency, we asked Brown to check into a small hotel in New Westminster and to see what arrangements he could make. Then we would meet him and bring along the five hundred dollars.

Since we would be working in Canada, we again contacted our old friend M/Sgt. Jack Purdy of the RCMP. Postal Inspector Carl A. Hoyer, who had the case, and I went to New Westminster, Canada, to contact informant Brown.

We didn't meet Brown in the open because he was afraid someone might associate him with us. The day after we checked into the hotel, Brown slipped a note under our hotel room door, reporting that he was to meet Duhamel on a certain corner at 1:00 P.M. the following day to make a "buy" of stolen money orders. We met a few blocks from the hotel the next morning and handed him the marked five hundred dollars.

M/Sgt. Purdy set up arrangements at the Port Coquitlam RCMP detachment for assistance in making an arrest as soon as Duhamel had sold Brown the stolen orders. M/Sgt. Purdy and the other RCMP had reservations about the setup. One RCMP officer remarked, "I'll bet you never see your stool pigeon or the five hundred dollars again."

At the time, we were wondering if he might be right. We really didn't know Brown very well. What bothered us was how he had spent time for trying to make a fast buck before we knew him; his specialty had been con games and fraud. So far as we knew, he was never a burglar. But what made him valuable was the fact that he had met many convicts during the times he was in jail and could talk their language and gain their confidence. He operated like a spy.

On Thursday the RCMP stationed radio cars within a few blocks of the corner where Brown told us he was to make the buy. We had all agreed that as soon as the deal was made, Brown would walk south along the street, carrying his hat in his hand. The RCMP were then to close in and arrest Duhamel. As U.S. officers, we could not make an arrest in Canada.

One o'clock came and nothing happened. The RCMP couldn't find Brown anywhere. One of us was stationed across from

Duhamel's home, watching to see if he came home. The other officer was across from Duhamel's sister's house.

About 1:30 P.M., after walking south, carrying his hat, and seeing no one, Brown called the RCMP office to find out what had happened and to ask why we hadn't picked up Duhamel. He had completed the buy. Not wanting to touch the money, Duhamel had Brown put the five hundred dollars in a small jar. Then he gave Brown the money orders and drove off in a small Morris car.

It took some while to find out what had happened. As it turned out there were two identically named street intersections in and near Port Coquitlam. It was our luck that the RCMP were waiting near the wrong intersection while Brown and Duhamel were doing business at the right time of day well over a mile away at an identically named intersection.

M/Sgt. Purdy, after receiving Brown's call, called all police cars in the area, asking that the Morris car be stopped and Duhamel brought to headquarters. In response to the call, an RCMP corporal stopped the Morris car as it was nearing Duhamel's house, left the car where it was, and brought Duhamel in.

Duhamel was searched but had no money on him. Until someone could be sent back to the Morris car to look for the five hundred dollars in a small jar, there were some worried law enforcement officers in Port Coquitlam. As soon as the money was found, Duhamel was the only one worrying.

Duhamel pleaded not guilty, and the preliminary hearing was held in the courtroom on the second floor of the old stone courthouse building. Informant Brown took the stand and testified how he had come to Port Coquitlam to contact Duhamel about buying stolen United States postal money orders. He told the court that a price of five hundred dollars was agreed upon and that the place and time for the exchange was set.

Anyone in law enforcement will tell you that informants rarely testify in open court. For one thing, they usually have a prison record, and so their testimony can be discredited. For another thing, an informant hesitates to testify because the underworld has always taken a very adverse attitude toward stoolies.

Brown was questioned in court about certain letters written

between the Duhamels, one of whom was in prison in the United States. He was asked to explain the code that was used. Although the defense attorney questioned him at length about this, he gave testimony that the simple code indicated that not only did Duhamel have United States stolen money orders but that he, along with his brother, were the ones who stole them from a U.S. post office.

Post offices are not usually prime targets for burglars. Very little money is kept overnight in any of them. Stolen postal money orders can be made out and cashed, but without the proper equipment that is hard to do.

Many of the smaller post offices throughout the land are located in a corner in a grocery store, where there is only one safe to accommodate both post office and store valuables. The safe is usually kept in the post office enclosure because both merchants and burglars know that when a safe in the post office section is broken open, the offense becomes a federal case. This means postal inspectors join local law enforcement officers in the investigation.

Many burglars absolutely refuse to enter the post office section of a building they have broken into because they don't want federal officers in on the case. Nevertheless, most courts will rule that if a building is entered that contains a post office, the case can be prosecuted in federal court.

When the automobile gained general use in the 1920s, bank holdups, post office holdups and burglaries, and crimes of a similar nature increased drastically. The automobile made it possible to make quick getaways and to commit crimes far away from where the burglar might live. Many small gangs were formed, consisting of from five to six men, only two or three of whom might go out on any given job. Generally they lived in the smaller western cities where the local law enforcement officers didn't bother them as long as they behaved themselves at home and committed their depredations at some distant point. This gave some burglar gangs a sort of haven and a place they could spend their loot and feel comfortably free from harassment.

Of all the gunmen of the late 1920s and early 1930s who sped about the West in fast cars, holding up banks in small towns, J. H. ("Blackie") Audett is probably the sole survivor.

When Blackie was barely sixteen, he and four others held up a mail train near Calgary, Canada. The heist, which netted over half a million, was the biggest mail-train robbery that had ever been pulled. Blackie never had much chance to enjoy his cut. He was arrested two days after the holdup. The gang had used Blackie's car, and tire tracks left at the scene of the holdup were easily traced. This was Blackie's first holdup and first arrest—the start of many that followed over the fifty-six years he made his living behind a gun.

The last time Blackie was arrested was on June 7, 1974, two days after he and three others held up the Ballard Bank of Washington in Seattle. Blackie's share was little more than $250, and he didn't use much of that cut either. Blackie was seventy-two and was capering with twenty-two-year-old Dennis Patrick Nolan and twenty-seven-year-old Angel Vargas. Still, Blackie wasn't the oldest one in this gang. The fourth man named in the complaint was Gerald Peabody, age seventy-four, who was described as armed and dangerous.

Between his first and last stickup, Blackie no doubt led a very interesting life. From available information, Blackie held up a mail train only once. The rest of his activities were devoted to small bank stickups and payroll holdups. He worked with those who have to be classified as "the best in the business." He is said to have worked with John Dillinger, Homer Van Meter, Charles ("Pretty Boy") Floyd, and Lester M. ("Jimmy") Gillis, also known as Baby Face Nelson. Blackie apparently never knew Bonnie and Clyde, but he did join the Fleagle brothers when they took a steel-plant payroll at the gate of the Colorado Fuel & Iron Company smelter in Pueblo, Colorado. This was before the Fleagle gang held up the First National Bank in Lamar, Colorado, and committed brutal murder in the process. It was truly a black day in Lamar, and Blackie was lucky to be far away on the day that holdup was pulled.

Blackie was a cool cat, and small jails in the West seldom held him for long. Big prisons simply offered more of a challenge. He was one of the very few who ever escaped from McNeil Island Federal Penitentiary, which is located on an island in Puget Sound surrounded by strong tidal currents.

Blackie engineered two escapes from McNeil. Once he got away in a speedboat that belonged to the warden. The second time he took a prison boat after first deactivating the prison siren that sounded when there was any attempt at escape.

The only prison that really held Blackie was Alcatraz, where he served time with other high-risk prisoners, such as Al ("Scarface") Capone. Lawmen said Blackie had jackrabbit blood; he was always running away.

Over the years Blackie's associates died by lawmen's bullets. John Dillinger, Homer Van Meter, Bob Brady, Wilbur Underhill, Bob Steele, Jake Fleagle, and Pretty Boy Floyd were all killed by lawmen. In the face of all this, Blackie remained a pure recidivist. He never changed. The pure love of excitement held his interest long after he knew he was too old for the game.

I was a young man growing up in Colorado on May 23, 1928, when the First National Bank at Lamar was held up. I will always remember that feelings ran high against the brutal men who held up the bank. When it later developed that Jake and his brother Ralph Fleagle were two of the four men who committed the crime, the very name of Fleagle carried connotations of evil in the area for years.

Bank bandits and holdup men were not new to this area. In fact, they were sometimes secretly looked upon with envy and often in sympathy in those depression days. Lamar, Colorado, is on the Arkansas River just south of Kit Carson and along the old Santa Fe Trail where the first pioneers trod on their journeys to Taos and Santa Fe in old Mexico. This part of Colorado is a hard country, where self-preservation has not always been easy. It was once the headquarters of the famed Mountain Men.

It was not at all surprising, then, for Newton Parrish, the president of the bank, to reach for his revolver and open fire on the four men who burst into the Lamar bank with guns drawn. His son, J. F. Parrish, went for a rifle, but both were immediately killed by the holdup men. The senior Parrish had hit one of the men in the jaw before he was cut down.

The holdup men scooped up twenty thousand dollars in cash and two hundred thousand dollars in U.S. Bonds and other negotiable securities, took two bank employees as hostages, and drove off at a high speed on Highway 50 toward the Kansas border.

Sheriff L. E. Alderman and his deputy were soon after the gang, but the desperados fired at the sheriff's car with rifles and succeeded in damaging the motor. The sheriff and his deputy, armed only with revolvers, were helpless to do anything more to stop the escape.

The Lamar bank holdup occurred in the days before there were "hot pursuit" laws, and many holdup men made dashes for state lines or county lines before the police could catch up with them. In those days, most lawmen had no authority beyond their state or county border. The need for some new law enforcement was urgent because the new highways and fast automobiles made escape for hoodlums too easy.

These conditions were ready-made for a man named J. Edgar Hoover. He took full advantage of the situation. He asked for and obtained jurisdiction for the FBI in the investigation of crimes against banks and interstate flights to avoid persecution. He built an empire, an efficient one that was to stifle rampant crime.

When the Lamar bank was held up, there was really no specific federal agency that could step in and coordinate a nationwide investigation badly needed to solve the crime. After the holdup, the Banker's Association named Hugh D. Harper, chief of police at Colorado Springs, to head the manhunt.

Dr. Hubert Work, a resident of Pueblo, had been postmaster general in 1922 and had a great deal of confidence in the work of postal inspectors. He had also been a personal friend of Newton Parrish, the slain bank president. He asked that postal inspectors be assigned to assist Chief Harper, particularly since they could work across state and county lines. Inspector Charles W. Pfaf-

87

fenberger was assigned to head up an investigation, and Inspector Maurice Clark and others assisted him. It was to be two years before the case was fully solved.

After the Lamar holdup, the desperados crossed over into Kansas and holed up in a horse ranch. Their first problem was how to get medical attention for the man who had been shot by Parrish. Dr. W. W. Weininger in nearby Dighton, Kansas, was brought to the ranch on some pretext. Of course, when he saw the nature of the wound, he knew he was in trouble. After he had treated the bandit, the doctor was taken to a lonely canyon and his head almost blown off by a shotgun blast by a man who was later identified as Jake Fleagle.

Jake rolled the doctor's body off a cliff and then pushed his car after him. In the process, Jake left a bloody fingerprint on a window of the car. This was the only tangible clue the law officers had to work with. Copies of the fingerprint were circulated widely, and a copy was sent to the Federal Bureau of Investigation's fingerprint laboratory.

The first break came in March 1929, when three persons were arrested in Stockton, California, on suspicion of the holdup of the Tracy, California, post office, where three registered letters containing twenty-seven thousand dollars for the local bank were stolen. The three could not be identified as the ones who had held up the post office, but one of the bandits was described as a thin man with a long-barreled pistol who shot at the postmaster's feet when he demanded the currency shipments. Their fingerprints were taken, and the three were released. One of the three gave his name as William Holden.

A few months later, on June 22, 1929, a Southern Pacific mail train was held up near Pittsburg, California. In this case, as in the Tracy case, a thin man with a long-barrelled pistol shot at the feet of the railway mail clerks while demanding that the registered mail be turned over. The holdup men were after a steel-mill payroll of two hundred thousand dollars, which wasn't on the train, and they had to settle for sixteen thousand dollars. The similarity in the jobs started a hunt for William Holden, and an inquiry found several aliases, including the name Jake Fleagle.

In checking over Holden-Fleagle's fingerprints, the FBI laboratory man noticed something very familiar in the pattern of the right index finger. This bothered him for several days until he finally linked it with the Lamar bank holdup fingerprint on Dr. Weininger's auto. Jake Fleagle was at last identified as being one of the principals in the Lamar bank holdup.

The rest of the case wasn't easy, but it did progress steadily. The Fleagle family was found living near Garden City, Kansas. Jake's mother and father were living there with one brother, Fred Fleagle. All had large sums of money in the local bank but had no visible means of support because their homestead was not productive. They said that Jake made money on the stock market and sent it to them.

Postal inspectors watched the mail coming for the Fleagles, and when a letter arrived from Kankakee, Illinois, bearing a post office box number, they waited for a person to pick up mail at Kankakee. The person who came to get mail out of the box was Ralph Fleagle, Jake's brother. Ralph was taken to Colorado Springs, where he denied for weeks any knowledge of the Lamar bank job. Finally, hoping to get a deal, he did tell Prosecuting Attorney Byron Rogers that his accomplices on the job were George Abshier, Jake Fleagle, and the bandit who had been shot in the jaw, Howard Royston.

Eventually Royston was arrested in San Andreas, California, and Abshier in Grand Junction, Colorado. Questioning of the three by Inspectors Pfaffenberger and Clark resulted in a full admission of the Lamar holdup. The three went to trial, were found guilty, and hanged in the Colorado State Penitentiary July 1930.

Jake Fleagle still remained at large. Jake was more careful than the others. Any letters he mailed he would post on a railway mail car so that it would not be possible to trace his whereabouts by a postmark.

It is illegal for postal inspectors, or anyone else, to open first-class mail, so the inspectors did the next best thing. If a letter came for a friend of Jake's, they sometimes were on hand when it was delivered, and then they questioned the recipient. Finally, one old accomplice of Jake's decided to cooperate when he received a letter from Jake, who wanted to know if the man would meet him in Yellville, Arkansas. The letter asked the man to insert an ad in the Wichita, Kansas, *Eagle* if he was interested. The man placed the ad and received another letter from Jake, setting up October 14, 1930, as the date they would meet.

About fifty law enforcement people were recruited to help take Jake into custody. They thought Jake might board the train before it reached Yellville, and eight men were assigned to ride the train. Fleagle got on at Branson, fifty miles out of Yellville. As soon as he was on the train, he was told he was under arrest and to raise his hands. Instead, Jake reached beneath his bib overalls. But before he could pull his gun, he was shot. Jake still managed to put up a fight before he was handcuffed.

As soon as he was subdued, he received medical attention, but he died the following morning.

Jake Fleagle's fingerprint matched the lone fingerprint he had left in blood twenty-nine months before on Dr. Weininger's automobile window.

To be effective, burglary investigations demand the cooperation of many different law enforcement agencies. As a result, associations of law enforcement people have been formed, and meetings are held to compare notes. During the 1950s and early 1960s, I belonged to quite a number of such organizations, including the International Association of Chiefs of Police, the Oregon-Washington Lawman's Association, the Northwest Check Investigators Association, and others.

Some cases are solved by the unusual evidence that remains at the scene of the crime to lead a trail to the door of the burglar, who thought he was in the clear. One such case took place in the snows of early winter, deep in the heart of Alaska.

This was the fate of the flying trapper who wasn't satisfied with his limit of beaver pelts. Trapper Joe, as we'll call him, ran a trap line with his brother near McGrath, Alaska. Trapper Joe tended the trap line in a small ski plane he borrowed from a friend in McGrath. The small frozen lakes where the beaver traps were set served as landing fields.

Trapper Joe came down too hard on a lake one day and broke

one of the skis. Grounded, as it were, he hiked several miles to the small town of Medfra, an old mining camp. Clint Winans's trading post and post office was in Medfra. The six or seven white people and three score natives were most friendly, and Trapper Joe accepted their hospitality for seven days while waiting for a new ski to arrive for his borrowed airplane.

Hanging around the store, Trapper Joe couldn't help noticing the informality and the fact that Clint never locked his safe or used spare keys to the store, which were left handy on a shelf. He used only the one on his key chain. Trapper Joe picked up one of the keys when no one was watching; it wasn't missed.

When the new ski for the plane arrived, Joe put it on and flew back to McGrath. A month or so later, when Joe and his brother had their limit in beaver pelts, Joe set out in the plane late in the evening to pick up the traps.

The next morning Postmaster Winans opened the door of his trading post to find the safe door wide open and sixteen hundred dollars missing, sixty dollars of which was post office money, which made the case a federal caper. Winans wired the U.S. marshal at Fairbanks, who sent Deputy Marshal Steve Mikulas to Medfra on a bush plane to make an investigation. Then the U.S. marshal, Stanley Nichols, notified me, the only postal inspector in the Territory of Alaska at the time.

When Deputy Mikulas reached Medfra, he soon found there was little to indicate any of the local people were responsible for Winans's loss. He talked to the people, and one little old native woman pointed out that there were many snowshoe tracks made by people coming into Medfra and going back into the bush. But, she said, "One man used white man's pointed snowshoes!"

The little old native woman reasoned that the man who had burglarized Winans's trading post and post office had come to town using a snowshoe built differently from those used locally. All the local natives and whites made their own snowshoes, and they were oval in shape.

"Outside snowshoes made different," reasoned the little woman. And to make her point, she followed the strange snowshoe tracks and found they took her to a nearby lake where a ski plane

91

had recently landed. There was no doubt in her mind the burglar flew in by night, took trader Winans's money, and flew away. He needed snowshoes to get from the lake to the trading post and back to his plane. Deputy Mikulas was convinced; local people in the bush rarely steal from each other until there is great need.

Then Mikulas had a little talk with trader Winans, who, after reflecting on the past few weeks, remembered the stranger who had stayed with him a month before while waiting for a new ski to come in for his plane. He remembered the man's name, Trapper Joe. Deputy Mikulas then flew to McGrath to talk to Trapper Joe, only to find that the trapper and his brother had left for Fairbanks.

By the time Deputy Mikulas had returned from his trip, I had flown to Fairbanks from Juneau. Together we tried to find Trapper Joe in Fairbanks. We couldn't find Joe, but we did find his brother, who seemed unaware of any burglary and surprised to have a visit in his hotel room from two law enforcement officers. He told us Trapper Joe had left for Seattle that same morning on Pan-American Airways.

Joe's brother went over the activity of the two for the previous few days, telling about Joe's trip to pick up the traps and his return the next morning. When he returned, Trapper Joe complained to his brother that the ice had been soft the night before on the lake where he had landed and that he had been forced to wait overnight until it had frozen solid again. Joe and his brother packed their gear and their limit of beaver pelts and made ready to fly to Fairbanks. He then mentioned that Trapper Joe had stopped off in Nenana on the way into Fairbanks to mail a package. The brother didn't know what might be in the package, but Joe had addressed it to himself, general delivery, Seattle. Trapper Joe had told his brother it was some personal things he didn't want to be bothered with when he flew to Seattle.

We called the postmaster at Nenana, and he remembered that a stranger had dropped in and had mailed an airmail parcel to Seattle. The Nenana postmaster said it had gone out the day before, and we determined that it had actually been dispatched on the same Pan-American flight that Trapper Joe had taken.

I alerted the postal inspectors in Seattle and gave them the details. They were on hand when Trapper Joe came to ask for his mail at general delivery in Seattle. When he arrived and had been handed the parcel, they stepped up with a warrant and asked Joe to open the parcel. What was in it? A few personal things and the money taken from Winans's trading post, including the post office money.

Trapper Joe said his brother knew nothing of the burglary. He related how he had planned the trip, landed on a small lake near Medfra, took some borrowed snowshoes that had been made in the States, and during the night went to the trading post. Using the key he had stolen at the time he was enjoying the hospitality of Clint Winans, Trapper Joe easily opened the door of the trading post. The safe was never locked, so he was able to clean out all the cash he could find—both Winans's money and post office money.

The airplane Joe and his brother had been using was rented. Joe told the inspectors he had always wanted a plane of his own, and he felt that the sixteen hundred dollars he took at Medfra, along with the money he would get from the sale of the beaver pelts, would make a nice down payment. Instead, the trapper earned a stretch of free board and lodging at McNeil Island Federal Penitentiary, courtesy of a federal judge after Joe had pled guilty.

Surprisingly, it is sometimes possible to use the talents of expert burglars. On August 12, 1964, the postmaster at the faraway, isolated post office of Yakutat, Alaska, called Seattle to report he couldn't get open his old 1930-model safe.

In such remote villages in Alaska, time leans lightly on the villagers, and there is rarely a real emergency that time won't heal. In this case, in the safe there was a registered letter containing cash to send two native youngsters to school in Oregon. If they were to get to school in September, some steps would have to be taken to open the safe so the registered letter could be delivered. A case entitled "Assist postmaster in opening jammed safe" was assigned to Postal Inspector M. C. Nelson, who was leaving for Alaska on general investigative work at the time.

Inspector Nelson, who was one of the younger men, told me he didn't know anything about opening safes. Of course, he would never have become an inspector if he had any real experience in the rip, peel, punch, blow, torch, or other illegal methods employed to get into a safe. He said he had read the bureau's publication titled *Burglary Investigation,* which covered many situations and procedures but was totally silent on just how to get into a safe. No other handbook covered the task. There wasn't much help I could give him. I mentioned two such cases I had had. In one case we had to get a maul and break the safe open from the back. In the other case, it was simple. I just turned the dial three notches and it opened. The postmaster told me that he had always opened the safe that way. I wondered why he had asked for help at all.

What to do, what to do? seemed to consume most of Inspector Nelson's thoughts, although he had many cases with him that presented much bigger problems. When the young inspector reached Juneau, he had two hours of layover between flights. There he stopped in to visit Chief of Police J. P. ("Pat") Wellington, who listened sympathetically. Together they contacted a Juneau safe man who said he couldn't get away for a week or so. He, too, was unable to give much instruction without viewing the safe. It didn't help when he commented, "Inexperienced people can work on a safe for days without getting it open."

Then Chief Wellington came up with an idea. He remembered there was a man in the city jail who was charged with bad checks, safecracking, and several other antisocial activities. Since the man had opened a number of safes illegally, he just might help with the problem—if he would talk. We'll call him Leroy.

They visited Leroy at the jail, and after hearing the inspector's story, he said, "I don't like to admit it, but from what you tell me, I am sure I can get into that safe in less than five minutes."

When asked if he would accompany the inspector to Yakutat, he said he would be glad to get out of jail for a while, take a free airplane ride, and perhaps pick up some additional pointers that might help him if he ever got back into the burglary field.

Authorities were contacted, arrangements were made, and the

inspector signed out for an accountable prisoner that had to be returned the same day. Efforts to arrange for a small bush plane to fly to Yakutat from Juneau were complicated by bad weather. It was late in the day when the burglar, along with some tools of his trade, was handcuffed to the inspector and taken to the seaplane float for departure, complete with screaming siren.

Upon arrival in Yakutat, they were met by Joe Brantley, a state game and fish official, who drove them to the Yakutat post office.

When Leroy, the professional, examined the safe, he found the locking mechanism had dropped to a point where it was believed impossible to open unless it was torched or peeled. The burglar said the rivet at the end of the spindle rod had crystallized and was broken. There was no one to dispute him. Leroy thought the best way was to peel it, which he did in less than five minutes. They had been in Yakutat less than an hour, most of the time spent in locating tools needed by burglar Leroy.

Leroy was apologetic about damaging the safe and assured the inspector that if the safe had been in good condition—just a simple lockout—he could have opened it without damage. He didn't say how.

When they had flown back to Juneau, Inspector Nelson offered to take Leroy to the Baranof Hotel Bubble Room for dinner. Leroy demurred, saying that if he was seen around town in the company of a law enforcement officer, it would be a severe rap to his reputation. He said, "Just take me back to jail, it's been a nice day."

Other burglars work hard at their trade. Joseph Romain Paul Beaulieu gained this reputation after leaving a twenty-five hundred-mile trail of smashed safes extending from Wilderado, Texas, through California, Oregon, and Washington. They called him the fastest ax in the West.

Surely this ax-wielding Paul Bunyan should have been easy to catch. The police handbooks read, "No burglar can enter any premise without leaving some clue, at least a *modus operandi* (M.O.), a method of operation."

The fastest ax in the West certainly had an M.O., he chopped the safes open with an ax, but he never hit twice in the same town until he was finally caught.

All the evidence pointed to a big brute of a man who was methodically chopping his way westward through a forest of small post office safes. Looking upon the havoc, irate postal inspectors bent every effort to catch him before the postal service ran out of replacement safes.

Most burglars fit into a sort of pattern. They have their methods, and law enforcement people can usually tell where they live, the kind of cars they drive, their names, and other bits of information about them. But the fastest ax in the West just didn't fit into any professional burglar book of records. He was a loner unknown to any of the gangs.

No, this Paul Bunyan didn't have a history. No one knew who he was, where he came from, or where he might strike next. One thing, he had to keep busy because he never realized much monetary gain out of any of the small post office safes he chopped open.

The M.O. was well established, and warning circulars were issued and sent to all law enforcement authorities and postmasters in a three-state area. One of them finally paid off, but only because this chopper made the mistake of returning to Creston, Washington, a small town where he had burglarized a post office a month earlier.

One night the town marshal at Creston noticed a meek small man who weighed less than 135 pounds come out of the schoolhouse carrying an ax. Could this possibly be the Paul Bunyan the post office inspectors wanted so badly? The marshal stopped him and found a post office typewriter and other things in his car that had been stolen from post offices.

Little Paul Bunyan admitted the chopping raids. He had hacked his way through twenty-five post office safes and claimed his fastest chopping time was about ten minutes. Thus ended the trail of the fastest ax in the West.

6

Murder by Mail

UPON FIRST VIEWING the demolition caused by the explosion of a bomb, most of us would think there was no evidence left that could possibly lead to the apprehension of the person who mailed the bomb.

Jilted lovers and others bent on revenge allow hate to blind good judgment and sometimes decide the way to satisfy their vindictive impulse is to mail the object of their hate a homemade bomb.

Attractive as this may appear to a person whose love has turned to unrequited hate, it is not a good idea. From the standpoint of getting away with premeditated murder, there is a better chance if a gun is used as the instrument of death. Certainly a gun is far more accurate. Bombs that are mailed may never reach the intended victim; the chances of doing so are about one in eighty. Records show that out of about 160 bomb mailings over six years, only two resulted in the death of the intended victim, although innocent persons have been seriously injured or killed when the mailed bombs explode.

Mailers stand an excellent chance of getting caught. Twenty or more years ago, investigations took a great deal of time, little physical evidence was gathered or developed, and most of the cases were solved because of persistent investigative work and a lot of luck. In recent years all this has changed. Now at least 80 percent of the major bomb mailings are solved, some within a few days, others within weeks. The belief that a person cannot be traced if they are not at the scene of the crime when a bomb explodes is a fallacy.

The Pasco, Washington, and the Lorain, Ohio, bomb cases give testimony that postal inspectors have developed highly successful sophisticated procedures in bomb-mailing detection in recent years.

Both the Pasco and Lorain cases were motivated by hate. In the Pasco case, the bomb was mailed to kill a judge who had previously sentenced the mailer for burglary. In the Lorain case, the bomb was mailed to kill a rival in a love-triangle case.

Washington State Superior Court Judge James J. Lawless was instantly killed the afternoon of June 2, 1974, when a small package he received through the mail exploded in his chambers when he opened it.

Postal inspectors, the FBI, police from Pasco and adjoining cities, officers of the sheriff's office of two counties, and members of the Alcohol, Tax, and Firearms agency all responded immediately. The fatal instrument had been mail, and, of course, the postal inspectors had primary responsibility. Inspectors M. L. DeVere and L. P. Love worked continuously on the case until it was solved.

Suspects in the case were numerous. The judge had been on the bench for seventeen years, and over the years he had had to make serious decisions that could have motivated a personal vendetta by any number of people. In addition, there were the radical groups who had claimed credit for bombings in the area.

From a field of at least one hundred suspects, the painstaking investigation by postal inspectors, assisted by other law enforcement people, got under way. The investigation finally centered on twenty-two-year-old Ricky Anthony Young of Prosser, Washington.

Judge Lawless had once sentenced Young for burglary. At the same time, the judge dismissed a kidnapping charge of abducting a fifteen-year-old girl, but he ordered Young to have no personal, written, or telephone contact with the girl for one year. The judge was killed by the bomb three days before Young was to again appear before him for a probation revocation hearing.

98

The kind of evidence developed in this case would have been lost without meticulous attention to the smallest detail. It was determined the instrument used was a homemade pipe bomb. About 170 bags of debris from the judge's chambers were gone through. A partial latent fingerprint of Ricky Young was found on a small piece of paper that had originally been part of the bomb wrapping.

Young was then charged in federal court with "causing to be delivered unmailable matter with intent to kill or injure." He was also charged with first-degree murder in Franklin County, Washington. Later the federal charges were dismissed to avoid any question of double jeopardy. Young was found guilty July 17, 1975, on the state charge of murder. The major portion of the testimony was given by postal inspectors and personnel of the Inspection Service Crime Laboratory.

The Lorain, Ohio, bomb case happened six years before the Pasco bombing. On July 8, 1968, a blast shook Don Ronec's mother's home in Lorain. Police and firemen who responded found the remains of a young man who had been killed in the explosion. When it was found the device had arrived through the mail, postal inspectors were called.

Along with the Lorain police, the inspectors began the meticulous task of going through the debris and then tracking down the killer. The letter carrier who delivered the parcel was able to remember delivering a brown cylindrical parcel about six inches long and which was closed with a metal screw cap.

In this investigation there were far fewer suspects than in the Pasco case. A love-hate motive was suspected early in the investigation, which pointed toward Orville E. Stifel II of Cincinnati, Ohio. Stifel had previously gone with the girl Don Ronec was to marry. But he had a reputation of being a model young man, and at first nothing definite existed that might implicate him.

Several damaged pieces of material were recovered from the scene of the explosion. The metal top of the container, along with a mailing sticker, part of the cardboard cyliner, and a piece of tape were sent to the Inspection Service Crime Laboratory, along with samples of articles found in a supply room of the company where Stifel worked.

Using the new atomic process called neutron activation analysis, the laboratory was able to report that the bomb fragments came from identical articles in the storeroom. This evidence, along with other testimony, satisfied the jury beyond any reasonable doubt of the guilt of Stifel. He was sentenced to life imprisonment.

Stifel's case was taken before the Sixth Circuit Court of Appeals, which held that neutron activation was a fully tested type of analysis. The case was then further appealed to the U. S. Supreme Court, which upheld the appellate court's decision. The Lorain case was considered to be a landmark case in that it represented a genuine advance in scientific identification.

The value of the crime laboratory is vital in the solution of almost every bomb case. This was demonstrated in 1962, when on March 18 a bomb exploded in the San Francisco, California, Airmail Field Post Office. The explosion injured two clerks and caused considerable damage.

Fortunately, there was an identification laboratory in San Francisco under the direction of Postal Inspector James V. P. Conway, who at the time was one of the outstanding document analysts in the United States. He had been called as an expert witness on numerous important cases of national interest, including the Dave Beck and Lindberg kidnapping cases.

As soon as the report of the explosion reached the laboratory, Conway and other personnel went to the Airmail Field Post Office. They found that mail near where the bomb had exploded appeared to have been penetrated with very fine shreds of what first appeared to be metal. After examination, it was found that these particles were finely shredded newspaper. After the debris was gone through, it was possible to piece together enough segments to find that the newspaper was from a copy of a daily paper that was printed in Chicago.

The mail that contained the bomb had arrived at the post office from Saigon, Viet Nam. It was little trouble to find that a certain U. S. Army Captain in Viet Nam received a daily paper from Chicago. Of course, the newspaper used to wrap the bomb could have been picked up by any one of several in Viet Nam. Questioning the captain eliminated the necessity of going further. He was returned to the United States for prosecution.

From that time on, more sophisticated methods in the investigation of bomb cases continued to be developed.

Some very strange and peculiar things often get into the mail. Parcel post may be opened for inspection, but it rarely is. All too frequently parcels do break open, and the surprise is often greater than opening a Jack-in-the-box.

Goodies are fine, but imagine the surprise of a startled postal clerk in Ketchikan, Alaska, who dumped a sack of mail and out tumbled a broken parcel loaded with high explosives. Dumped out of a poorly wrapped parcel onto the workroom floor fell ten blocks of army demolition explosives in two-inch-by-two-inch-by-eleven-inch forms, two boxes of primer caps, a military riot bomb, smoke bombs, eight cartons of blasting fuse, a quarter pount of TNT, and two cans of blasting caps. Experts estimated the total explosive force as equal to 134 pounds of TNT.

This was not a nice thing to have in the mail, in the building, or even in town. Nervous postal employees called the Coast Guard, who removed the explosives and took them out of town to an ammunition bunker. The postal inspectors were called.

There was really no investigation needed. The person to whom the parcel was addressed was located in Anchorage. He turned out to be a young man who had been on a demolition squad in the army. When he was discharged, he had managed to appropriate the conglomeration of explosives. Instead of planning to start some sort of armed uprising, he said he planned to build a home and wanted the explosives for blasting out a foundation. He appeared to be truthful in this respect, reluctant to tell how he had come into possession of the material, but totally surprised that there was any objection to his mailing explosives.

Why did he mail them? It was simple; he planned to drive to Alaska over the Alaska Highway, and he suspected that the stuff was too dangerous to be hauled in his auto over that rocky road.

His reasoning was certainly sound on this point, but we wondered if he thought the postal service transported mail on some magic carpet.

He had mailed the parcel at Pasco, Washington, addressing it to himself in Anchorage, Alaska. It was put on the Northern Pacific mail train at Pasco and first dumped at the Seattle Terminal Annex. The terminal annex is a large three-story building where hundreds of postal people work. Handling of mail at the terminal annex is not necessarily done with tender, loving care. The mail passes over belts and goes down chutes between floors not designed to move high explosives. If the parcel had detonated there, the building would have been ripped apart.

The parcel was then loaded aboard the *S.S. Fortuna* of the Alaska Steamship Company, along with other mail for Alaska. Why it happened to be taken off at Ketchikan is an unanswered question. Probably it was put in the wrong sack by an employee who certainly would have used more care if he had had any idea at all what he was handling.

The young man was charged with mailing explosives at Pasco but was allowed to enter a plea of guilty in Anchorage. The judge was not too sympathetic to the young man's professed confidence in the U.S. Mail Service and sentenced him to serve time in the Anchorage jail.

Occasionally when a person is sentenced for a crime he will threaten to get the judge, the district attorney, the arresting officer, or all three. Rarely are such threats carried out, but the chance is always present. Being sentenced can be a very traumatic experience.

A few years ago, Frank R. Freeman was United States attorney for the Eastern District of Washington at Spokane. As such, he had prosecuted many criminal cases. To his knowledge, he had never been threatened by anyone.

One Saturday afternoon he was sitting at home alone, watching a football game on television. He heard the mailman come by, and during a break he went out to pick up the mail. He was surprised to find a small parcel in the mail addressed to him with the return address of Norman Sheridan, who was special agent in charge of the local office of the Secret Service.

102

By coincidence, it was Freeman's birthday, but he was certainly not expecting a birthday present from the Secret Service. It was also near Halloween, so he became doubly suspicious.

He studied the parcel, which was about the size of a one-pound candy box, noticing the crude hand-printed address. He took the wrapping off slowly and gingerly, tightly gripping the box inside. Nevertheless, a rattrap inside was sprung, but the full force was blunted by Freeman's grip on the box.

Shaken, he found the parcel contained a rattrap set to detonate twelve wartime blasting caps, which were intended to explode a fist-size piece of dynamite. If the homemade bomb had gone off, he would have probably been cut in two at the waist. Frank Freeman called the postal inspectors. This certainly wasn't a thing that should have been in the mail! Freeman's suspicion of a prank because of his birthday or Halloween had saved his life.

The inspector's job was to find the man who had mailed the bomb. Attorney Freeman had no idea at all. Special Agent Sheridan could hardly be considered a suspect.

The first break came when the inspectors talked to Federal Judge Charles Powell. He remembered receiving a small American flag soiled with excrement shortly after he had sentenced a young man in a selective service case some six months before. The boy was serving time and could not have sent the bomb. However, upon hearing of the conduct of the boy's father in court when his son was sentenced, the inspectors became curious.

The father was a potato farmer living in nearby Deer Park. Since the address on the bomb parcel was hand-printed, the inspectors visited him and asked for some samples of his writing and printing. He voluntarily furnished some hand-printing to clear his name. Far from clearing him, the document examiner positively identified the father's hand-printing as being the same as the hand-printing on the bomb parcel.

Still not satisfied, Postal Inspectors Kenneth W. Luke and Robert Parrish delved further into the case. In time they were able to locate the post office clerk who had accepted the parcel. When they talked to him, he was able to remember and describe the man who mailed the parcel with accurate detail. Arrangements were made for the clerk to again observe the suspect, and he was able to positively identify the mailer, who was the father of the boy Judge Powell had sentenced.

The father engaged Carl Maxie, an astute criminal attorney, to defend him. Maxie asked for a bifurcated, or two-part, trial. The first part of the trial concerned itself with the criminal offense, and the jury returned a verdict of guilty. The second part of the trial was to determine if the father was "able to tell right from wrong at the time of mailing the bomb."

Two psychiatrists testified that the offender was temporarily insane at the time he mailed the parcel but that subsequent electrical shock treatments had corrected the condition. The jury accepted the opinion of the psychiatrists, and the father walked out of the court a free man, "no longer a threat to society."

Inspectors always enjoy the full cooperation of other law enforcement officers, and consequently they continually provide all the assistance they can to others in this field. The bombing of the Meier and Frank Department Store in Portland, Oregon, is a good example of this cooperation.

At 2:30 P.M. on Friday, April 15, 1955, a blast shook that department store. The explosion demolished the men's rest room on the third floor of the store. Amazingly, no one was hurt seriously. A janitor in the hall and a woman across the street were cut by flying glass and debris.

When the blast occurred, Aaron M. Frank was in the process of reading the following letter that had been brought to him by a clerk in the store who had found it on the desk of the Lost-and-Found department.

ATTENTION: Aaron M. Frank

Read this carefully
and very thoroughly

By the time you receive this message or very shortly thereafter there will be an explosion take place in your store. This explosion has been brought about to convince you that the writers of this message are dead serious about the demands and instructions contained therein. This first explosion has been designed to do a minimum amount of damage. Whereas, the second explosion, if you permit it to happen, is designed to do the maximum amount of damage. We have concealed in your store charges of explosives that are (outside of (nuclear) weapons) composed of the most powerful explosive material that can be obtained.

These high explosives have been attached to a very accurate timing device. These explosives will go off some time during the 12-hour period which ends at 12:00 o'clock noon, Saturday, April 16, 1955. We have spent several months in setting up and planning and perfecting this entire thing. We have also gone to considerable expenses so as to make certain that there is no possibility of error in any of our planning, explosives or timing device.

Aftermath of bomb explosion in the men's rest room of the Meier and Frank Department Store in Portland, Oregon, April 15, 1955.

If and providing you follow, to the exact letter, the following instructions one of us will contact you by telephone and we will reveal to you where these explosives are concealed so that any further damage to your store and its contents can be avoided. If you do not follow these instructions, you will not hear from us again and we will have no alternative but to let these explosives go off and we know that they will do damage far in excess of the demands that we have placed upon you.

You may take one other person into your confidence. This person must not be a member or previous member of any law enforcement body or of any detective agency, which includes any of your store detectives.

HERE ARE YOUR INSTRUCTIONS: You will, as rapidly as possible, get together in cash of United States currency the amount of $50,000 (Fifty thousand dollars) of which not more than one half shall be in $20 bills and the remainder in $5 and $10 bills. This money you must place in a light colored suitcase. This suitcase must not be any larger than what it takes to hold this amount of money.

You will now have the party you have chosen place a carnation in their coat lapel, where it will show, take this suitcase, packed with the money and go stand next to the curb in front of the Imperial Hotel, 410 S.W. Broadway, between the hours of 6:30 P.M. Pacific Standard Time and 7:00 P.M. of this day, Friday, April 15.

At 7:00 P.M. you, or the person you have entrusted with this mission, will go directly to the Bell Telephone attendant offices, 728 S.W. Washington Street, where they will go to booth number 15 and await a telephone call which will give them their further instructions. Either you or the party you have selected as your confident should have on their person at least $50 in cash and your instructions to follow the orders that they will receive.

Do not be foolish and think that you can find the explosives for you would only be endangering lives and gambling time.

Also you must restrain yourself from notifying any law enforcement agencies until after the money has been delivered and you are notified as to where the explosives are hidden. Do not make the mistake of trying to equip the contact man with any type of concealed radio transmitters or have him followed. He must also be unarmed. Do not endeavor to mark this money in any manner for if you do anything at all to have uas apprehended until after you have been notified as to where the explosives are concealed we will call off the entire thing and let our explosives do their worst. There will be only one of us who will meet your contact man and if anything should go wrong and he should be apprehended we are pledged that the remaining shall continue to systematically conceal explosives in your store that will eventually make it dangerous to open your doors to the public.

Remember, you are to keep the contents of this letter from all news reporters and police until after you have been notified as to where the explosives are hidden.

If, for any reason, you think this is a bluff all you have to do is fail to follow any of these instructions and we can promise that you will regret it to the upmost. For, remember, you are vulnerable in more ways that we care to mention. You have our solemn promise that you will never be bothered again by any of us if you cooperate.

If you follow these instructions and stick strictly to the time schedule you will have nothing to fear, as you will be notified in plenty of time to enable you to prevent these second explosions. The key word for identifying ourselves on the telephone is:

S.K. FLINT

Misspelled or improper words are exactly as contained in the original extortion letter.

The extortion note had warned Aaron Frank not to notify any law enforcement agency until the money had been paid. This was impossible, as the store was invaded by members of both the fire and the police departments within minutes after the blast.

Frank gave the extortion note to Portland Chief of Police James Purcell, Jr., and William D. Browne, captain of detectives. He told them he could see no alternative to paying the demand of the extortionist. If only he were involved, it would be different, but he had to think of the hundreds who visited his store daily. He did agree, however, to let the police make the contact. He immediately gathered fifty thousand dollars in small bills from throughout the store, put the money in a suitcase, and handed it over to the police.

The instructions of the extortionist reflected unusually thorough planning. The contact was to stand outside the Imperial Hotel near the curb during a heavy traffic hour, which would give the extortionist a good chance to look him over.

Rather than risk the identification of any of the better-known experienced city detectives, a rookie patrolman named Leines was selected. The captain told Leines he would be on his own, but that he might have an opportunity to pass a message by putting it in an empty cigarette package and throwing it away. He was to be followed by experienced men as closely as possible.

Leines was off, dressed in a suit, wearing a carnation in his coat lapel, and carrying fifty thousand dollars in a small suitcase. He stood at the curb in front of the Imperial from 6:30 P.M. until 7:00 P.M., then went to the telephone offices on Washington Street. At about 7:08 P.M., the telephone rang in booth fifteen. When Leines answered, a man told him to return to the Imperial Hotel, where he would find a note under the seat in the third telephone booth.

At the hotel, Leines found a baggage-locker key and a typewritten note taped to the underside of the seat. The note instructed him to go to the train depot and open the baggage locker. There Leines found another note instructing him to hire a taxi and go south toward Eugene at twenty-five miles an hour until he saw three flashes of a headlight behind him. He was then to stop the cab, set the suitcase on the shoulder of the road without leaving the cab, and ride on for five miles.

After reading the note, Leines casually shoved it in his pocket and into a cigarette package that contained only one cigarette. As he went through the depot waiting room, he took the package out of his pocket, removed the cigarette, lit it, crumpled the package, and tossed it into a sand urn.

A detective who had been watching had a porter clean out all the sand urns in the depot, to avoid identifying any particular one, and bring the contents to him. The police then knew how the payoff was to be made. Unmarked police and sheriff's cars were instructed to pass the slow-moving cab at frequent intervals.

Leines rode in the cab for the five hours it took to reach Eugene. Here he asked the driver to pull up at a phone booth, where he reported that no signal had been given and that he was returning to Portland. The attempt to catch the bomber when he picked up the fifty thousand dollars in the suitcase had failed.

From here on the case would take a lot of hard work.

The large store was closed until the next Monday, and a thorough search was made for explosives. None was found. Experts examined the rubble left in the men's washroom and reported the explosion had been caused by about ten sticks of dynamite set off by a common fuse that burned perhaps fifteen minutes before detonation.

At that time dynamite was sold in almost every rural grocery or hardware store in the state. All these had to be checked to find out if any stranger had purchased dynamite. The typewritten extortion notes were sent to the FBI laboratory for analysis, along with other bits of evidence picked up. The FBI reported that the notes had been written on a Royal Standard typewriter, one of about three million that had been made of that model.

Interviews of many persons who had been in the store, as well as others who came in to volunteer information, had to be made. There were reports that a blind man led by a dark-haired woman had been seen in the vicinity of the washroom shortly before the explosion, but the description was vague. The possibility of a blind man being able to accomplish all the necessary steps taken from the actual bombing to the possible pick up of the extortion money on the highway seemed too remote to consider seriously. It was felt that the bomber had probably disguised himself as a blind man in order to allay suspicion or identification.

As if the investigation were not enough, the publicity inspired others to attempt similar schemes of extortion. Seven or eight persons were arrested, which entailed considerable police work. None of those arrested could be tied to the Meier and Frank case.

In most cases of major importance, the solution of a crime is often resolved through the willing cooperation of other law enforcement people. This case was no exception.

Postal Inspector Stanley Smoot worked closely with the Portland police in joint investigations involving burglary and theft of mail from street letter boxes. The police gave him a photostatic copy of the bizarre extortion letter. It developed that Inspector Roland Severtson had been investigating a Portland jeweler in a mail-fraud case for the sale of fictitious sales contracts to a bank and other lending agencies. It just happened that the total amount of false contracts held by one of the finance companies was fifty-one thousand dollars. If that amount could have been raised immediately, the jeweler might stave off exposure. It occurred to the inspectors that the fifty thousand dollars demanded in the extortion letter might be more than a coincidence.

Inspectors Severtson and Smoot related their suspicion to the police and furnished copies of typewritten material the jeweler had written. However, none of the material could be identified as similar to the typewriting on the extortion notes. The matter was then set aside for the time being in the press of other work.

It is always the mark of a good investigator to keep in mind small details that someday might fit into a pattern. It was nearly eight months before things began to fit together. In another fraud case, a relative of the jeweler was involved. Inspector Severtson had the case, and as he laboriously went over massive amounts of typewritten correspondence, he came upon the strange word *up-most*.

Inspector Severtson had demonstrated before that he was gifted with a retentive memory. The inspector remembered the use of the word *upmost* in some document he had seen eight months before. Something clicked and he reached for the old files to take a look at the Meier and Frank extortion note again. Sure enough, there was the word *upmost*. The note read, in part: "We can promise that you will regret it to the upmost."

The papers the inspector was going over was correspondence typewritten by W. C. Peddicord, a blind man. Inspector Severtson contacted Inspector Stan Smoot, who substantiated his suspicion. The two took the new evidence to the Portland police. When the material was compared with the original notes, the coincidences became even more apparent. Since the FBI had made other analyses of evidence, the material was sent to the FBI laboratory.

On December 15, Captain Browne called to tell the inspectors that the Peddicord letters had been positively identified with the extortion notes. That same afternoon, the inspectors showed the police where Peddicord lived, and they participated in his arrest and questioning. Peddicord, a thirty-nine-year-old blind man with a wife and five children living at home, readily admitted he had perpetrated the extortion-bombing plot and was able to repeat the extortion letter almost verbatim, although its contents had never been published.

Peddicord's failure to follow through and make contact with the payoff messenger was not "blindman's buff," according to Inspector Severtson. It was because of an argument with his woman accomplice. His accomplice reportedly told him she did not expect such a violent blast when the charge went off and refused to continue in the plot. He was unable to arrange for other transportation.

Ironically, Peddicord lost his eyesight when he was nineteen years old in an explosion when he was dismantling a refrigerator and the refrigerant exploded into his eyes. Over the years he had tried through sensationalism to bring public attention to his condition, which would often result in donations out of pity for him. Once he hitchhiked from Portland to New York for a cornea transplant that wasn't a success. In 1939, he applied for the job of executioner at Sing Sing Prison when he learned there was a vacancy. He and his dog scaled the sheer and treacherous Beacon Rock in 1938, the second-largest monolith in the world.

Aaron Frank had offered a twenty-five thousand-dollar reward for the arrest and conviction of the person who had bombed his store. After Peddicord's arrest, many persons stepped forward, asking for the reward—none of whom had identified Peddicord as the bomber prior to his arrest and admission. In fact, some of them had previously identified some other person entirely.

Peddicord was sentenced April 20, 1956, to serve twenty years in the state prison at Salem, Oregon, which he said was too severe.

The postal inspectors could not share in the reward because they were officially employed by the Post Office Department at the time, and cooperation of this nature is considered part of their duties. Needless to say, Aaron Frank was very happy the case was closed and called the chief postal inspector to express his profound relief and gratitude. The reward more properly went to those police officers who worked long hours on their own time from April to December in their efforts to solve the case.

Smut Merchants

IF ANTHONY COMSTOCK were alive today, he would probably be in traumatic shock. As it is, he should be spinning in his grave.

Comstock was a young activist crusader against obscenity in the period following the Civil War. He made such a favorable impression on certain members of Congress that in 1873 he was appointed a special agent, post office inspector. He served with considerable success in keeping the mails free of pornographic material until his death in 1925.

Since 1865 there had been a federal law against mailing obscene material which was punishable by a one-hundred-dollar fine and/or not more than one year imprisonment. Comstock was active in getting the statute revised to make the penalty a felony, punishable by a five-thousand-dollar fine and imprisonment of not more than five years. The law was changed in 1873, and Comstock was appointed to enforce it.

Comstock has long since been laid to rest, but the statute prohibiting the mailing of lewd, lascivious, or obscene matter is still being enforced—probably not as vigorously as it was in Comstock's day or, for that matter, as vigorously as it was in the 1960s.

In 1958 the law was again changed to permit initiation of prosecution at the point of delivery, at any point in transit, as well as at the point of mailing.

Dirt for money's sake has long attracted professional pornographers who find a ready and eager market. In the 1960s, the

Portland *Oregonian* carried an article that estimated panderers of pornography had an annual take of two billion dollars. Two thousand million dollars a year is a great deal of money, even today.

The ever-moving line that separates pornography from acceptable literature makes it difficult to put any figure on smut. Certainly smut peddlers are no longer depending on street-corner sales of French postcards.

Even Supreme Court justices, as old and experienced as they must be, have trouble staying with a definition. In 1957, they decided that "if the dominating theme of material, taken as a whole, appeals to the prurient interest of the average person when contemporary community standards are applied," it is obscene.

This was a legal cop-out, leaving the decisions up to each community, whether it was sophisticated, jaded, or prudish. What might be obscene in rural Idaho was probably acceptable in Hollywood.

It is impossible to pick up a newspaper or magazine, tune in a radio or television program, hear a panel discussion, or spend an evening in conversation with friends or associates without being made aware that we are undergoing a social revolution. Reading matter and pictorial periodicals that twenty years ago were handled "under the counter" and made available only to adults or persons known to bookstore operators are now displayed as regular items on news racks for the purview and purchase by all—juveniles included. The material which was then considered to be too racy for display is generally considered mild by our current standards, and stories depicting sex in slang terms and in many deviate forms are standard fare. There are groups active in our society that maintain that the open presentation of this material to permit freedom of choice by the public is intended under our constitutional system.

We frequently hear eloquent defenses for obscene matter and attacks on the investigative services through charges of censorship or possible violation of the constitutional right of expression. Numerous court decisions have maintained that obscenity has no constitutional privilege.

A few years after passing the obscenity statutes, on March 3,

1879, Congress decided to allow a special low-rate subsidy to newspapers and periodicals that disseminated information of public character or that were devoted to literature, sciences, or the arts. This was called a second-class permit.

Certainly Congress had no intent that a second-class subsidy would ever be used in pandering smut. Nevertheless, it was inevitable that a two-billion-dollar industry would be tempted to test the mailability of borderline pornography.

The first national magazine of wide circulation to get into trouble was the prestigious *Esquire* magazine. By the year 1944, *Esquire* had gained a reputation for being "colorful" for that day and time.

Postmaster General Frank C. Walker was convinced that *Esquire* had stepped over the line. He revoked the second-class privilege of the magazine on the grounds that it was not being published for the dissemination of information of public character. He didn't say it couldn't be mailed but merely took away a subsidy that represented about five hundred thousand dollars in postage charges. The postmaster general said, "Such writings and pictures may be in that obscure and treacherous borderland zone where the average person hesitates to find them technically obscene but still may see ample proof that they are morally improper and not for the public good. . . . A publication which uses them in that manner is not making the special contribution to the public welfare. . . . I cannot assume that Congress ever intended to endow this publication with an indirect subsidy and permit it to receive at the hands of the government a preference in postal charges of approximately five hundred thousand dollars per annum."

This sudden blow was not taken lightly by *Esquire*. Its publishers claimed the postmaster general's order amounted to censorship and went to court. The case was heard in Washington, D.C., and on July 15, 1944, the judge ruled that the postmaster general had acted within his powers and that his act amounted to classification of mail, rather than censorship.

The judge said, "The postmaster general was warranted in taking the view that Congress meant for second-class mail (newspapers and periodicals) to be a contribution toward public education.''

Esquire lost this battle but eventually won the war and had its second-class permit restored. Postmaster General Walker exhibited fortitude in taking on one of the largest publications in the country, but he was criticized in some circles for doing his job.

As a result of the final ruling, others were encouraged to do as much pandering as possible without stepping across the invisible line that has become progressively bent toward a more tolerant view of what constitutes lewd, lascivious, or obscene matter.

Hugh Hefner of *Playboy* magazine became most critical of some of the views of postal inspectors when he felt his right to make a living in the way he was doing it might be affected. This is easily understood when it is considered he was making a fortune.

Ralph Ginsburg published *Eros* magazine and the *Housewife's Handbook on Selective Promiscuity*. Ginsburg even went so far as to send questionable advertising to personnel in the United States attorney's offices during a subscription drive for *Eros*.

In the early 1960s, Postmaster General Lawrence F. O'Brien decided that if anything positive was to be achieved in fighting pornography panderers, it had to take place in the courts. He told postal inspectors that criminal action should be sought in all obscenity cases.

At that time Ginsburg was publishing *Eros* and other publications that were flagrantly erotic. He was indicted and brought to trial. At the trial, both he and Edward Mishkin were convicted of violating postal obscenity statutes. The case was appealed, but Ginsburg's conviction was upheld in a 5-4 Supreme Court decision in March 1966. Justice William J. Brennan said that the publications were permeated with the ''leer of the sensualist.'' The salacious material was marketed upon that basis alone, with no redeeming literary value.

This did not stop Ginsburg or others for long, but they saw a lucrative enterprise threatened. Ginsburg tried to reestablish *Eros* but eventually settled for a periodical called *Moneysworth*. In his advertising he billed himself as ''Crazy Ginsburg.''

In the earlier 1960s, postal inspectors were causing the arrest of nearly one thousand persons a year for violation of the obscenity statutes. Since there is considerable money involved and a ready market for the product, a number of the cases were challenged and taken to higher courts. All sorts of litigation chipped away at controls until a great deal of anything in the way of pornography, in the mails or outside, goes unchecked.

In the 1960s as many as fifteen postal inspectors devoted their entire time to investigation of obscenity violations. Of course, hard-core pornography is still investigated vigorously, but some of the other violations do not receive the attention they once did.

Dealers in hard-core pornography rarely use the mails, and the FBI investigates interstate transportation by private carriers. How some X-rated films are allowed to be shipped is questionable.

Today deviates of every kind seem bent upon advertising their particular thing. Most of these cases are no longer investigated so long as the particular fetish is kept reasonably private, but many feel compelled to advertise. When complaints are made, postal offenses are still investigated, and the cases are presented to the U.S. attorney in the district where mailings are made or received.

In the book-publishing business, the mere publicity of having a book banned is a boost to its sale. Advertising by adverse court action made the book *Tropic of Cancer* a best-seller. *Lady Chatterley's Lover* and *Fanny Hill* were other books that faced litigation, gained recognition as a result, and became best-sellers.

Two other books that didn't make it so big were *Hillbilly Nympho* and *Sex Kitten*. Judge J. Erwin Shapiro of the New York Supreme Court reviewed these two books and said there was no pretense of literary merit. The books were "profane, offensive, disgusting, and plain, unvarnished trash," he said. Nevertheless, he refused to call them obscene.

There has always been the underlying concern that pornographic material sales advertising is frequently slanted for the juvenile. Juveniles do constitute a large bloc of the market, and racy pinups, nude art films, and books of so-called sex instruction are purchased by them.

Parents are sometimes at a loss to know how a pornography dealer obtains the names of their children. Often the name is obtained from a mailing list compiled by firms advertising otherwise innocent things such as radio kits, model airplane designs, or other items that attract youngsters to reply to ads appearing in national magazines.

Some children, upon receiving advertising for obscene material, order it in the hope they can intercept the mail before their parents see it. One girl, who worked in the principal's office at her high school, had the mail sent to her at school. Unfortunately, the seller's promise to send the material in a "plain unmarked envelope" identified the matter almost as well as if it had been labeled "Pornographic Material." The large envelope bore only her address and a post office box return. School officials, possibly familiar with this type of mail themselves, intercepted the mailing and turned it over to the girl's parents.

Those who wish to avoid pandering mail advertisements may go to the post office and have the mailer stop sending such material under the Anti-Pandering Act.

Over the years mailing of obscene pictures and material by groups of husband-wife-swapping "swingers" and by others whose fetish involved bondage or flagellation were investigated upon receipt of complaints. We once arrested a man the U.S. attorney called the "Rubber-Goods Man." He had trunks full of all types and kinds of rubber goods, from wading boots to raincoats. His was an odd fetish, but somehow he felt he should advertise it by sending pictures of an obscene nature to others, some of whom objected.

We arrested a prominent doctor in a Montana town who, along with his wife, belonged to a wife-swapping group. On weekends they traveled to other towns to experiment. They mailed pictures of an obscene nature back and forth. When he was confronted with the pictures and envelopes used, his guilt was at first denied. Unfortunately, the doctor had an unusual ring he wore on one of his fingers. The ring was displayed prominently in some of the obscene photographs that had been mailed.

The United States attorney for Montana was not inclined to prosecute until the doctor's wife visited him in his hotel room in an effort to persuade him not to prosecute. That mistake helped him make up his mind, and he filed charges against the two. The court punishment was not nearly as severe as the blow to the doctor's reputation. He had to close his office and move away.

Permissiveness and the enchantment with sex has tended to move the American public far away from the Puritan morality of prior times, but literary agents of large publishing houses now report that the popularity of the books where obscenity is the dominant theme is starting to wane.

The story of the critical shortage of women in the early days of Seattle has been told many times. To adjust this imbalance, Asa Mercer made a trip back East and sweet-talked a whole boatload of women to come to Seattle, promising them matrimony.

The girls arrived by steamship, and it was a great day in Seattle. For decades it was a distinction to be known as one of the Mercer girls or as a descendant of one.

Bringing the Mercer girls to Seattle was a benevolent act by one of the city's founders. There have been many matrimonial schemes throughout the years, some of which were anything but benevolent. One such interesting case dates back to September 18, 1944, when Lilli Michler was arrested in Chicago on a charge of defrauding at least eleven men out of thousands of dollars in a matrimonial scheme worked by her.

Lilli and her husband, Paul Michler, left Germany in 1929 and lived in Canada until 1932, when they entered the United States.

The two learned that there were many Germans who had come to the United States after 1923 who were in the market for a German *Hausfrau* who could cook and who possessed some worldly goods. In their efforts to meet such a person, they frequently answered blind ads appearing in the personal columns of German-language newspapers. Some would insert ads themselves, requesting correspondence from women who were interested in matrimony.

Lilli would answer these ads, and, after some correspondence, she would meet her victim (or "mark"'), practice her culinary art and other accomplishments. In at least four cases Lilli went so far as to "marry" the victim, but usually she was able to relieve the anxious swain of his money before it was necessary to enter into the sacred bonds of matrimony.

The way Lilli would accomplish her lonely hearts swindle was to first gain his confidence, then to persuade the lamb whom she was about to fleece to rent a safe-deposit box in which both of them would put all their money. Lilli had one maneuver that would encourage her victim to do this. When she was alone in a room with the victim, Lilli would withdraw six one-thousand-dollar bills from her bosom to demonstrate her good intentions.

"My eyes stuck out, I never saw a one-thousand-dollar bill in my life before," one of the victims told postal inspectors. He was quite willing to put the few thousand he had saved, along with Lilli's six thousand in a safe-deposit box. As soon as Lilli felt the coast was clear, she would take all the money out of the joint safe-deposit box and disappear.

The Michlers operated for a long time before victims complained to the postal inspectors. Since the mails had been freely used in the scheme, it was clearly a mail-fraud case. The Michlers used different names in each case and kept their whereabouts concealed. They traveled by auto and were believed to be operating between Chicago and Milwaukee. Wanted circulars were posted in that area, and within three days a tip came in that resulted in their arrest.

The scheme had worked smoothly because the marks were all eager for marriage and were easily blinded by Lilli's cooking ability, her feminine charms, and her thousand-dollar bills. Each was a victim of his own cupidity, and when they suddenly realized what had happened, many were too embarrassed to complain.

In fact, most people who have been bilked prefer to take their losses and keep it to themselves. To do otherwise would only direct public attention to their own greed or stupidity.

Husband Paul Michler was believed to be the brains behind the scheme, which was executed with typical German thoroughness. He remained in the background, didn't use the mails, and, although he was arrested with Lilli, the case against him had to be dismissed.

Lilli entered a plea of guilty in Chicago and was sentenced to serve ten years at the Women's Federal Penitentiary at Alderson, West Virginia. Shortly after she entered the penitentiary she escaped with the assistance of her husband.

Paul certainly stood by Lilli throughout. Before the case came up, he attempted to bribe one of the victims with five hundred dollars not to testify against his wife. However, after assisting in her escape, they were again apprehended, and this time Paul was sentenced to two years for his efforts in the escape.

The Sir Francis Drake Case was a good example of the way many people react even when they are taken for their total life's savings.

Sir Francis Drake was an English admiral who sailed around the world in the sixteenth century. He was a leader in the defeat of the Spanish Armada in 1588 and raided the Spanish main in his ship *The Golden Hinde*. By records of his exploits it was presumed that he accumulated a considerable fortune.

When he died, his property was supposed to have been inherited by his brother, Thomas Drake; his relatives; and Queen Elizabeth of England. His wealth was deposited in the Tower of London, according to legend.

An imaginative American seized upon this bit of vague history as a basis of a scheme to do a little exploiting of his own. He induced almost two hundred fifty thousand greedy "pigeons" to donate two million dollars for the purpose of defraying the cost of litigation to free an estimated one hundred million pounds of the alleged Drake Estate. Sir Francis Drake would have admired such piracy.

A hundred million pounds back in 1936 when this scheme was operated would have amounted to about five hundred million dollars in U. S. funds, an unbelievable sum, especially in those days. Persons who contributed funds were promised their share of the dormant funds, money held by the Bank of England, property held by the Crown in various parts of the world, including the Redwood Forest in California.

On the face of it, one would assume it impossible that the Drake wealth could have remained intact and dormant for well over three hundred years. People named Drake, and those with relatives or ancestors of that name, were prime targets; but anyone could get in.

The suckers bit and, having been hooked, were too proud to even acknowledge that they had been "had," even to themselves. It looked like a case of simple mail fraud to the postal inspectors, but first they had to prove that the Drake Estate didn't exist.

Proving the nonexistence of something is often more difficult than finding the real thing. First a postal inspector visited England to look into the possibility of the alleged Drake Estate. He found that the inheritance had completely eroded and that whatever Sir Francis Drake had left was long since gone.

Eight persons who were operating the scheme were found guilty of mail fraud on January 31, 1936. A member of Scotland Yard and an English barrister were brought to Chicago to testify at the trial. It took three and a half months to present all the evidence.

It was difficult to get many witnesses out of the quarter million who had been bilked. The credulity of the victims demonstrated an almost childlike faith in the fantastic fairy-tale promises of the swindlers. Many had donated their entire life's savings and probably would have donated more after the trial if they were able. Many were very antagonistic toward the postal inspectors for investigating the case and proving that it was pure fantasy.

It has often been said that a picture is worth a thousand words. A Tacoma couple found a way to turn a picture into a thousand dollars, or more.

In a matrimonial swindle, they mailed photos of attractive girls to prospective swains as bait. Perhaps it was a matter of necessity, for the woman in the caper was anything but attractive. To send *her* picture to the most ardent suitor would have promptly cooled any development of romance. The man who investigated the case was Postal Inspector Edward E. Kellar, of Seattle, and this is the way he told it to me.

Things were tough for Earl and Nettie. It was hard work picking the crops in the Yakima Valley, and it didn't pay too well. They had their problems. Somewhere along the line, they began using the names Earl and Peggy Smith. Eventually Earl got a job with a carnival operator at Tacoma, who knew him as Earl Smith. Earl and Peggy moved into a trailer parked on the carnival equipment lot. A sort of homemade bankruptcy may have caused them to change their names.

In about 1968, Earl and Peggy opted for a share-the-wealth program; that is, they planned to share in the wealth of romantic and lonely bachelors looking for a mate. To do this, they listed Peggy in various lonely heart clubs, falsely stating that she was an unmarried young woman interested in matrimony. These ads were placed under the name Peggy Smith, using post office box addresses in Puyallup and Sumner, Washington; and General Delivery in Spanaway, Washington.

In this way, they came into correspondence with numerous men throughout the country who were interested in marriage and who seemed to think the grass was greener somewhere else. When a letter was received from a likely prospect, either Earl or Peggy would write, using the name Peggy Smith. Generally they would say that Peggy was a shy young woman, never married, and, in fact, a virgin; that she made a poor but honest living by baking pies in her home and selling them about the neighborhood. These letters would say she was waiting for the right man to come into her life. When she found him, they would be married and she would work very hard to make him a good wife. Earl wrote as many, if not more, of the letters as did Nettie; and to avoid any handwriting problem from letter to letter to the same individual, Earl would handprint his letters and Nettie would write in script.

They would enclose a photo with the first letter, indicating that it was a photo of Peggy. It most certainly was not a photo of Peggy. The girl in the photo was most attractive; whereas Peggy was plain—very plain.

At any rate, the mail moved swiftly (as it sometimes does), with letters going back and forth between Peggy and those whose wealth was about to be shared. By about the third letter, as you may have guessed, Peggy was madly in love and certain she had found the right man for her. There was only one slight problem. She didn't have money, for baking pies barely kept her an honest woman, and she would need some money to pay transportation expenses to come to her intended. Naturally, the ardent suitor would magnanimously offer to send money for travel expenses, which Peggy was somehow never able to refuse.

Plans would be made for Peggy to leave on a certain day as soon as the money was received. Then, when she failed to arrive at the scheduled time, most of the suitors would realize they had been prize chumps and would let it go at that, without telling anybody

Nettie Edris, also known as Peggy Smith, mailer of photographs of beautiful movie stars in a lonely hearts matrimonial scheme.

about it. Before long, however, one of the disappointed Romeos became genuinely worried when Peggy failed to arrive. He thought she surely must have met with some misfortune or foul play while enroute to him, and he began writing letters to the postmasters and other officials to try to find out what might have happened. The postal inspectors soon learned of the inquiries and recognized this as another matrimonial scheme.

You have to give Earl and Nettie credit for versatility, if little else. They could adapt their style of writing to fit the situation. They seemed to be able to tell whether a religious-type letter would be best or, in other cases, maybe a risqué letter. One individual got into a series of risqué letters with Peggy, and finally Peggy sent him a nude photo of herself. Well, as I said before, Peggy was a plain girl, but the fortunate thing was that the photography and lighting were poor. What the man may have thought when he received the photo and how he may have tried to reconcile it with the photo of the good-looking woman received in an earlier letter is difficult to imagine, but one can suppose he must have thought that baking pies is a hard way to make a living and really takes something out of a person.

One victim from New England was very diligent. Through a long series of letters he kept asking the most detailed questions of Peggy. He must have been the type of person who reads the fine print in a guarantee. At long last he apparently decided that this girl had everything, all in good shape and stacked in the proper order. So he sent the transportation money, only to wait in vain for a dream that never materialized. As careful as he was, I doubt that even Sears could sell him anything by mail now.

Another suitor had no money to send, so he sent none. He spiced up the investigation when he was found living in a stone cabin in the Missouri Ozarks with only a pet crow for a companion. The crow hadn't been out of the one-room cabin for about five years. Needless to say, the postal inspector kept his hat on and didn't sit down when he talked to this mark.

Another correspondent played it smart. He must have had some misgivings, for he sent the transportation money to the manager of the bus station in Tacoma, to be used only for a ticket. Earl and Nettie never did figure out how to beat that. Oh, well, you can't win them all.

After several interviews, the facts in the case were plain, and the matter was presented to the United States attorney, who could see it was a case of false advertising. In the interest of consumer protection, he filed mail-fraud charges against Earl and Nettie. Realizing that defense was useless, both Earl and Nettie entered pleas of guilty. Earl was sentenced to five years and Nettie was placed on probation for five years by a federal judge on March 20, 1969.

In matrimonial cases it takes two to seal a bargain, and a fellow named James Burt Coward operated on a big con scale. No small checks for transportation money satisfied him. Coward, with no visible means of support, lived in a comfortable home in San Antonio, Texas, with his wife and teenage son.

Realizing that the bulk of the wealth was in the hands of women and that lonely widows were prime targets, he went to work writing only to those women who revealed substantial resources. Never using his real name, Coward wrote charmingly romantic letters slanted to reflect interests and sentiments expressed in letters he received. He soon had his lady correspondents believing they had at last found a person they could be happy with.

The con artist worked on one mark at a time. These efforts provided him with an above-average income; he drove only new Cadillacs.

Coward charmed and married the unsuspecting without serious trouble until one of his victims swallowed her pride and complained to Postal Inspector L. B. Tyler in Phoenix, Arizona. This woman had answered an ad Coward had placed in a Los Angeles correspondence club publication under the name of Jarmand Bart Cravelyeh. Their correspondence blossomed, and Cravelyeh wrote that he had lost his wife, was lonely, and had Texas oil property. She encouraged him to visit her in Salem, Oregon; and when he did, she found him attractive, dignified, and attentive.

In a short while she decided to marry him, and he helped her with the sale of her home. The money was placed in a joint bank account. This, he explained, would make it possible to start test drilling on his ranch near oil wells that had already come in. He told her he had not been interested in developing the oil property for himself, but together they would become rich.

After a marriage in Tucson, they spent a honeymoon traveling. She had found her new husband all she could ask for until they arrived in San Antonio, Texas. Here she consented to withdrawing most of their funds from the bank. Cravelyeh left her alone most of the day in their hotel room, only to return in a fit of temper, accusing her of saying something to someone about the secret of his oil property which ruined all his plans.

He drew a gun, made her pack up, took her to the bus depot, and sent her back to Oregon. Back in Salem, she was without a job, broke, and worried. She had to live with friends. In time she realized that her husband had deserted her. She wrote the police in Los Angeles and San Antonio. They had no record of any Jarmand Bart Cravelyeh. Suspecting that she had been the victim of fraud, she told her story to the postal inspection service.

Inspector Alfred E. French was asked to check on Cravelyeh in Los Angeles. At the correspondence club he found Cravelyeh's application for membership, but no Cravelyeh. In the club records he also found applications from Jan Cartier and Armand Cary, names that somehow seemed to fit together. Another inspector in New York turned up the name of a Jan Bryk Cowart, who had married a woman he met through a Los Angeles club and had also taken her to San Antonio, where he threatened her with a gun and sent her back to New York after fleecing her of fifty-eight hundred dollars. If Cravelyeh, Cartier, Cary, and Cowart were not the same man, they operated in much the same manner. With this information, Inspector French began the tedious work of investigating these swindles.

He found that Cravelyeh had mentioned to the correspondence club that he wanted to buy a new typewriter. Inspector French visited typewriter sales shops from one end of the city of Los Angeles to the other, a seemingly hopeless task. Finally his per-

126

severance paid off. A dealer remembered a purchase, went through his books, and told French that Cravelyeh had asked him to mail his old typewriter to Mrs. Anthony Coward in San Antonio, Texas.

Inspector French's suspicions were well founded. Now he had Cravelyeh, Cartier, Cary, Cowart, and the key name, Coward. He also had an address. James Burt Coward was soon identified by two of the women as the man they had married and the one who had bilked them. Another finally agreed to testify. Coward had little choice but to plead guilty. He was sentenced to three years in prison.

But this wasn't the last the inspectors heard about Coward. Inspector French didn't think the man would give up such an easy and lucrative sham. One day the inspector learned that Coward had been found murdered and his body burned beyond recognition in Texas. This wasn't enough for either Inspector French or Sheriff Oliver Moore of Kerr County, Texas.

Sheriff Moore found that Coward and Jack Jordan had been together about the time of Coward's purported murder. Strangely enough, Jordan's mother had reported her son missing. The two men were about the same size. Suspecting that Coward may have killed Jordan and planted his own wallet and identification so that he could again be free to resume his lucrative matrimonial scheme, the case was pursued further.

Sheriff Moore and his men began to check up. Again by diligent police work they finally traced Coward to a motel near San Antonio. He gave up without a struggle. But while he was getting dressed, he took a dose of cyanide and died within seconds. The sheriff found that cyanide had also been used to murder Jack Jordan.

Women, and the world in general, have seemed to get along just fine without Coward, also known as Cravelyeh, Cartier, Cary, and Cowart.

8

Million-Dollar Junk

"SEND TEN CENTS FOR BIG MAIL, Box 23145 B Chicago, Ill."

Simple in its appeal, this advertisement frequently appeared in the weekly rural newspapers of the early 1900s. It brought promise of at least some mail to many who were lonesome in those sparsely settled territories before television or radio came along to entertain them and sell them soap.

When I was a small boy, I never received any mail in my own name, and this bothered me. It may have been because my mother was postmaster and I had seen the vast amount of mail some of the people in our small town did receive. Rather than be left out, I finally sent ten cents to one of the BIG MAIL advertisers, and the results were fantastic.

To this day I have never been without my fair share of direct-mail advertising, which has offered me all sorts of rare treasures, gadgets, and fantastic bargains I might otherwise have missed out on during a long lifetime. I like to get mail, and when people don't write to me, I know that some enterprising advertiser will not forget me. I think most people feel the same. When I sent my ten cents to Chicago long ago, I didn't realize my name and address would be indexed and entered on lists that would be sold to promoters and advertisers as a mailing list.

Possibly because of its central location, Chicago became the mecca of direct-mail advertising. Large mailing firms, such as the Le Marge Mailing Service, prepared and mailed advertising for almost any business or promotion.

If there was at least a 10 percent response to a mailing campaign, it was considered successful.

Mailing lists can be purchased for almost any purpose. In the early days there were few telephone books listing names, and people selling mailing lists were very happy to get the name of a sucker like me. The ten cents was only incidental.

In recent years, mailing lists have been built up from motor-vehicle registrations, license renewals, hospital-patient lists, credit records, senior-citizen rosters, motel and hotel registrations, charitable and religious contributions, health-spa visitors, church rosters, and endless other sources.

For a few cents a name you can buy a mailing list that is designed to reach those people likely to be interested in your particular product, promotion, or solicitation. There are lists designed to reach cancer victims, arthritis sufferers, and those who are seeking everlasting youth and beauty.

For years a great many advertisers have found it very profitable to use third-class mail to promote their business. With the continuing increase in postal costs for this class of mail, there is a growing question of how much longer this method of advertising may be able to last. But private mail-delivery services do not offer much latitude in reaching selective markets, nor do they deliver in the rural or isolated areas that are sparsely settled.

Third-class mail is called circular mail, bulk mail, box-holder mail, permit matter, and sometimes junk mail, a term discouraged by postal officials and totally disliked by the Associated Third-Class Mail Users.

Those who persist in calling it junk mail forget that direct-mail advertising has made millionaires of many enterprising people in our country. John D. MacArthur, who was the richest man in America before his death in 1977, got his start toward a billion-dollar fortune by selling insurance by mail under the name of the White Cross Insurance Co.

Most direct-mail advertising is sophisticated and offers merchandise that is just what it is purported to be in the advertising. Federal laws have been in effect for years to protect a public that has a great deal of trust in the U. S. Mail. Those who persist in making false claims about their products through the mails are the ones watched by the postal inspectors.

Charitable, religious, and patriotic organizations, in their drives to obtain funds, often engage professional mailing services. A man named Abraham Leonard Koolish was probably the originator of the idea of mailing unordered merchandise in the name of some charitable, religious, or patriotic organization. In 1915 A. L. Koolish began his mail-order business under the name of the K & S Sales Co. of 6227 Broadway, Chicago, Illinois. This expanded with numerous subsidiaries, including Garden City Novelty Manufacturing Co., Garden City Fabrics Co., Lincoln Novelty Co., Montrose Silk [stockings] Co., Chicago Mint [candy] Co., Pierce Tool and Manufacturing Co., [peanut vendors and handgrip measurers], Sally Astor Frock Co., Rand Sales Co., Rota Clock Co., Standard Distributing Co., and Granville Sales Co.

These "name" firms were used as needed, and all made mail-order sales of novelties and cheap merchandise by means of paper punchboards and other enticements.

Koolish and his associates successfully used the mails in various promotions from 1915 until the 1960s on a continuing basis. In the myriad companies formed to promote mail-order business and solicitations were many members of the Koolish family, sometimes acting behind the scenes. Often involved with father Abraham were son David Frank Koolish, brother Phillip Harry Koolish, and son-in-law Ralph E. Stolkin. Stolkin was married to daughter Ruth Koolish.

In addition to his Koolish connections, Stolkin built an empire of his own. His worth was estimated at nearly 3.5 million dollars in 1952. He was not as successful in other business deals though, and after he got out of the mail-order business, his attorney said, he lost his fortune and died a poor man.

By 1952, Abraham Koolish was a multimillionaire with an

estimated worth of $3,382,348.00 amassed from selling everything from coonskin caps to life insurance by direct mail.

In 1930 the Federal Trade Commission issued a complaint against the Koolish parent company, K & S Sales, for using punch-boards and lottery-type methods in the sales.

Strangely, nothing came of this official government complaint for seven years. Finally, the FTC held hearings and issued a cease-and-desist order in January 1938. Then, in about August 1939, Koolish was cited for violation of the cease-and-desist order against K & S Sales and paid a penalty of forty-five hundred dollars.

The cease-and-desist order failed to slow down the enterprising Koolish group. K & S Sales had been liquidated in January 1938, and Universal Industries at 2222 W. Diversey Ave., Chicago, Illinois, was formed, with George W. Ehrlich as registered agent. The same operations were then continued, using Atlas Industries, Inc., which was operated by Phillip and Marvin Koolish; Regal Industries Inc.; and Atlas Premium Co.

This time the FTC acted more quickly. It held a hearing late in 1939 that resulted in a cease-and-desist order issued August 24, 1941, against Universal. However, Universal Industries had been dissolved long before the order was issued.

From 1940, Abraham L. Koolish, Phillip N. Koolish, and George W. Ehrlich operated Westminster Life Insurance Co. and Westminster Life Insurance Agency at 2222 W. Diversey Ave. in Chicago, selling cheap insurance by mail. This was done at the same address that had been used by Universal Industries. After a net profit of about one and a half million, Westminster Life was purportedly sold to John D. MacArthur of Chicago in February 1946 for $305,000. Billionaire MacArthur had previously purchased Bankers Life and Casualty Company in 1935 for $2,500.

The next firm to blossom at 2222 W. Diversey Ave. was Empire Industries, incorporated on April 5, 1946, with M. E. Petty as the original president but with the Koolish family running the business. This firm enjoyed a long life, running until June 30, 1952.

Empire Industries sold great quantities of pens, auto-seat covers, raccoon-fur caps, silverware, and novelties through the mail under the guise of solicitations for charity. At various times son-in-law Ralph E. Stolkin appeared as president and treasurer, Phillip Koolish appeared as secretary and treasurer, and Abraham L. Koolish as operator of the business.

Postal inspectors learned that Empire Industries, Inc., was changed to a partnership, Empire Associates, on July 1, 1952, with Abraham, Phillip, and David Koolish along with Ralph E. Stolkin as partners. Then, on March 26, 1956, Empire became part of a newly incorporated La Marge Mailing Service Co., Inc., of 417 So. Jefferson, Chicago, Illinois.

Among the very remunerative operations well known to the public was the mailing of unordered miniature license plates attached to key chains, with an appeal for donations in the name of Disabled American Veterans, 1423 E. McMillin St., Cincinnati, Ohio. The name of the company making the mailings was the Ident-O-Tag Co. of Chicago, which was a partnership of Abraham Koolish, son Phillip, nephew Theodore, and George W. Ehrlich. During the year 1943 alone, eight million tags were mailed, and a reported 6 percent of the net profits were sent to the DAV. This went on each year until 1946, when the DAV purchased the right to conduct the mailings for $1,336,500. Abraham Koolish was retained as consultant at one thousand dollars a month until 1951.

The Ident-O-Tag idea was a winner and filled a need in the automobile-oriented world. The DAV found that in fiscal year 1949 under their own operation they made 1.8 million dollars profit, instead of the few hundred thousand they had been receiving a year when the program was a Koolish promotion.

Between January 1952 and November 31, 1953, Empire Industries, Inc., mailed about twelve million unordered pens and name stickers with requests for charity donations in the name of National Kids Day Foundation, Inc. Testimony was given before a New York State legislative investigating committee that almost $4 million were obtained from the public, but only $401,000 went to the charity.

Postal inspectors found that among those involved in the National Kids Day Foundation promotion were Abraham L.

Koolish, David F. Koolish, Ralph E. Stolkin, Leo Gans, and Richard Slayton.

The inspectors then turned up another amazing operation that took place in a short two-year period between August 31, 1952, and June 30, 1954. Empire Associates, Gayton Associates, Inc., Le Marge Mailing Co., Inc., and Dudley Sales Co., Inc., sent out millions of unordered pens by mail, good-luck pennies, and personalized name stickers with charity solicitations in the name of the National Foundation for Asthmatic Children. Appeal letters in this campaign contained such statements as: "$1.50 will just cover the cost of the pen—if you unlock your heart, you will unlock their lungs."

An audit by a CPA firm found it "appalling" that of the $762,060.14 collected, only $8,650 went to charity. It was also found that the National Foundation for Asthmatic Children was a very small private school in Tucson, Arizona, with a total capacity of about fifty children. All of those treated at the school, except twelve, were maintained by payments from their parents.

In still another promotion in 1954 the Empire Division mailed unordered personalized name stickers in the name of the National Foundation of the Blind, Inc., of 605 S. Few St., Madison, Wisconsin. The total collected from the public amounted to $1,737,612.99. Terms of the unbelievable agreement provided payment of $0.15 to the charity out of each contribution received of $1.25. Nothing was paid the charity if the donors sent in only $1.00.

In 1955, Empire Associates mailed about three hundred thousand unordered personalized name stickers in the name of the National Haven for the Blind, Inc., Washington, D.C. It was represented in the appeal that remittances of one dollar or more would be devoted almost entirely to welfare projects in aid of the blind and would become an endowment of the National Haven for the Blind. It was found that of the $24,849.09 collected, nothing was paid to charity.

The Handicapped War Veteran's case involved mailings of unordered personalized name stickers, fountain pens, and ball-point pens soliciting funds under false pretenses for handicapped veterans. A mail fraud conspiracy indictment was returned in Chicago on May 17, 1955, naming Empire Associates and others, including Abraham L. Koolish and David F. Koolish, as defendants. The defendants were notably successful in delaying court action, so much so that the case never did come to trial.

With a rich history of success in using the mail in many varied promotions, it was almost inevitable that the Koolish interests would one day visualize the potential in mail-order land sales of recreation and retirement lots.

Beginning in the 1960s, there was a land boom in the sale of recreation lots in the Southwest and West. The public was suddenly tired of the pressures of big-city living and wanted the supposed security of a little piece of land out West. Naturally, there was soon a host of land speculators offering subdivided lots by the thousands.

Mail-fraud statutes had been enacted as far back as 1871 to protect people from land-selling schemes when the West was first opened up, just after the Civil War. Both government and private land had sometimes been sold by people who didn't even own it. Most states had few or no public disclosure, land planning, zoning, or consumer protection laws that would prohibit anyone from buying a section or two of desert land, having it platted into city-size lots and then selling the lots.

In 1963 the postal inspectors had about 150 open cases for investigation of possible misrepresentations made in the sale of new subdivided land in the West. The century-old mail-fraud statutes seemed to be the only immediate way an unsuspecting public could be protected from these schemes if the mails were used in any way.

If you could dream up a scheme to have several thousand people each send you five dollars a month, you would have a sweet little thing going for you.

Many promoters did dream up such schemes and then put them into action. First, they would buy some cheap, almost worthless desert land, paying as little down as possible. The land would then be subdivided into lots, which would be offered for sale, sight unseen, by mail.

These schemes worked well because many people had faith in the mail service, were gullible enough to believe most advertising material, and had a desire to own a recreation vacation lot at a price they could afford.

One of the biggest land promotion cases we had was called Lake Valley. It developed that several men, probably financed by David Frank Koolish, had bought sixty-nine hundred acres of almost worthless land located about twenty-two miles south of Burns, Oregon, in the isolated four thousand-foot-high desert country for twenty-four dollars an acre, on time.

This land was subdivided into 566 lots per section, and the operators began to sell lots in two or three sections at $5 down, $5 a month until $385 was paid, plus 6 percent interest.

Development costs were ridiculously low. There was no high growth or other obstructions to block the surveyor's transit. After the lots, streets, and blocks were laid out and surveyed, a road grader scraped off the sagebrush along the streets. Street-corner signs were put up, and a small vacant A-frame sales office was built on the property for show only. A large billboard on the site announced the sale of lots at Lake Valley.

The developers felt they had an inalienable right to sell land, and the county assessor, Dale G. Ferris, had little choice but to sign the plat when it was presented, but he did endorse it: "Signed under protest on advice of county attorney."

Then came the advertising, by far the most costly part of the venture. Advertising was handled by Phillips and Cherbo, an advertising agency at 35 Wacker Dr., Chicago. This firm, according to Dun and Bradstreet, grossed two million dollars a year (1962).

Lake Valley, the name of the development, was probably selected because the land was located between Harney and Malheur lakes.

Phillips and Cherbo advertised the lots as the "Greatest new investment opportunity in the West."

The word *paradise* was liberally sprinkled throughout the full- and half-page newspaper advertisements seven times. The advertising campaign covered Hawaii, Washington, Oregon, Wisconsin, Utah, Idaho, Texas, Wyoming, Nevada, Colorado, and other states. They called their company the Harney County Land Development Corporation and set up an office in Burns, Oregon, where the buyers could send their money.

Advertisements were alluring with statements like: "Big game animals abound. . . . Thousands of antelope, deer, and elk roam the area. Pheasants, quail, partridge, and sage hens everywhere. . . . Waterfowl shooting at its best! . . . In addition, there is boating, waterskiing, golfing, swimming."

Pictures in the slick broadside that was sent out upon receipt of the first five dollars, or even upon inquiry, showed beautiful mountains, lakes, pack trains, and a shot of a camper frying freshly caught trout. Some of these scenes were nearly two hundred miles away from Lake Valley. The tracts of subdivided land, depicted as beautiful and fertile, were actually barren except for sagebrush and other plant life associated with the cold high-level alkali semidesert. Nearby was the 184,000-acre Malheur National Wildlife Refuge, but the refuge was always closed to hunting. Harney Lake was surrounded by alkali flats totally unsuited to water sports such as swimming or waterskiing. Fish could not live in the alkali waters of the lake.

Among other things, the operators retained 50 percent of the mineral, gas, and oil rights, which might be more than five hundred feet below the surface. This was based on rumors that there was oil in that area. They were selling lots in a sterile wilderness where freezing is probable almost any month of the year and winter temperatures have gone as low as twenty-five degrees below zero. Well water was of no value for irrigation. The nearest swimming was a pool at Burns, twenty-two miles away. There were stores, a hospital, and schools in the pleasant town of Burns, but nothing at all at Lake Valley.

Naturally, some of those who were hooked by the direct-mail advertising wanted to see what they had bought and made a trip to Lake Valley to savor the alluring charms depicted in the advertising. What they found was not what had been advertised.

The Harney County Land Developer's sign on the high desert country of Eastern Oregon in 1962. City-size lots offered for sale by mail. A Koolish enterprise.

Some stomped right up to the office in Burns and demanded their money back.

As the facts came together, it appeared that the operators had plans to gross 2.75 million dollars at Lake Valley before they were done.

Inspector R. A. Severtson of Portland, Oregon, was placed in charge of the case on October 10, 1962, when it became obvious the land was being misrepresented in the mail-order campaign. He was assisted by many other inspectors, including Earl J. Ingebright and Paul E. Moon.

Inspector Severtson and the others checked the facts and interviewed all the operators and the people who had complained. The case was then presented to U.S. Attorney Sidney Lezak at Portland, Oregon, for prosecution. It was a landmark case because it would determine whether modern day subdividers could use the mails to bilk the public. It would be the second such case to go to trial, although fourteen similar cases in the West had by then been investigated and were ready for trial.

Lezak eventually took the case before the grand jury on May 1, 1963, and indictments were returned against Abraham Leonard Koolish, who was then seventy years old, David Frank Koolish, John Milton Phillips, Jr., and Jack Cecil Cherbo, all of Chicago. Richard Dale Walker, an attorney, along with George Edward Isaacs and Arthur Hall, all of California, were also indicted.

After several months of legal haggling, a change of venue was granted and the trial was begun December 2, 1963, in Pendleton, Oregon. Three of the seven were found guilty after a lengthy, hard-fought trial. Two young attorneys assisted Lezak for the government. With apparently unlimited resources to obtain high-cost legal talent, the two Koolish men were defended by a prominent Portland attorney, William H. Morrison, and three others. Walker had two attorneys, and Isaacs and Hall had one apiece.

Walker, Phillips, and Cherbo were found guilty of using deceptive advertising in newspapers in order to obtain down payments on 1,394 sales of almost worthless Lake Valley land.

Phillips, Walker, and Cherbo appealed their conviction, and the ninth Circuit Court of Appeals reversed the convictions, stating that there was ample evidence to support the verdict but that U. S. Judge John F. L. Kilkenny erred in instructing the jury at the Pendleton trial.

While the three were awaiting retrial, they decided to plead *nolo contendere* (no contest) to the original verdict and were then fined forty-five hundred dollars each.

Although Abraham L. Koolish and son David were not convicted in the Lake Valley case, the Koolish empire was beginning to crack. Other charges were finally catching up with them.

On November 6, 1961, the Sister Elizabeth Kenney Foundation of 2400 Foshay Tower, Minneapolis, Minnesota, filed a civil suit in Chicago against the Le Marge Mailing Service, Abraham L. Koolish, David F. Koolish, Ralph E. Stolkin, and John Carnell to recover $2,685,000 and their own mailing lists. The suit alleged that twenty million dollars were collected from the public in a mail campaign operated by the defendants for the charity but that only eight million dollars were received.

This prestigious charity had entered into arrangements with the Koolish interests to raise money. Mailings of unordered Sister Kenny "seals" requesting donations in the name of the charity were made by Empire Industries, New Century Corporation, and the Le Marge Mailing Service, Inc., from 1949 until 1956.

On May 29, 1963, after a ten-month mail-fraud trial, a federal court jury in Minneapolis, Minnesota, found Abraham L. Koolish, David Koolish, John Carnell, George Zimmerman, and Fred Fadell all guilty of concealing about seven million dollars in collected donations they had made for the Sister Kenny Foundation. Marvin L. Kline, a former mayor of Minneapolis, had previously been found guilty of raising his own salary from twenty-five thousand dollars to forty-eight thousand dollars a year without authority while he was an officer of the charity.

The presiding judge at the trial was the now Chief Judge Edward Devitt. The case was prosecuted by United States Attorney Miles Lord, now a federal judge. He was assisted by Hartley Noreen, who is now a bankruptcy judge.

Abraham and David Koolish were both sentenced on September 13, 1963, to two five-year terms to be served consecutively, and they were ordered to pay a fine of seventeen thousand dollars and court costs.

John Carnell was sentenced to five years. He was paroled July 13, 1966. George Zimmerman was placed on probation for five years. Fred Fadell was placed on probation for one year. Marvin Kline was sentenced to serve two five-year terms.

Until the 1963 convictions, it could be said that the Koolish family and their associates had been inveterate mail-order operators never dissuaded by public opinion, investigations by government agents and better business bureaus. Cease-and-desist orders, postal-fraud orders, complaints, and even criminal indictments failed to do more than inconvenience them.

They simply continued to operate in the face of it all for the better part of forty years, doing their mail-order business under new names with different people as officers of their many subsidiaries, the names of which were frequently changed, which added to the difficulty of identifying the operations Koolish controlled.

In response to complaints received by the Post Office Department, many postal inspectors worked on various cases involving phases of the Koolish operations. Inspector Gilbert Flategraff of Saint Paul interviewed many of the principals, including John D. MacArthur, the richest of them all. It was Flategraff, along with inspectors Phil Frantz, Ray Newell, Lloyd Sundheim, and George Reis who investigated the Sister Kenny fraud that resulted in the Koolish empire downfall.

The Koolish enterprise and business acumen has to be admired. It occurred in an age when their operations were, to an extent, the expected way of doing business. Some of their ventures required a large risk of capital before any profit could be realized and some of their operations were entirely legitimate and legal. It all happened in an age when many fathers said to their sons, "Get it honest if you can, but get it!"

9

The Politicians

THERE HAS ALWAYS been an *esprit de corps* among postal inspectors that extends even into retirement. To a man, they are proud of their work, their fellow workmen, the force they work for, and their position in it. It is natural that jealousies arise, but when they do, they are normally brought about by investigative competitiveness or a desire for some promotion.

By virtue of their work, postal inspectors gain a great insight into the operations of the postal service. It is only natural that sometimes selections are made from the Inspection Service to fill specialized administrative positions within the postal service.

Prior to the days of the Postal Corporation, the Post Office Department was a very political body. In particular, postmasters and rural carriers were political appointees. All promotions and appointments to positions above the clerks and letter carriers could, on occasion but surely not always, require the benefit of political clearance.

If a postal inspector was promoted to an administrative position, particularly to a high one, the chances are he was probably recommended by a member of his congressional delegation. This was in the face of the nonpolitical status of inspectors that was so necessary if they were to properly and adequately make the investigations that could be relied upon, no matter what political party was in power. However, the Inspection Service usually had a great deal to say in the selection of those they felt would be best qualified to fill a specific vacancy.

Strangely enough, the much-criticized and maligned political system did produce well-qualified leaders as a rule. The system did offer the chance for the weeding out of the incompetent with every change of administration, which is something neither the civil service nor the new corporation has been able to do.

Many postal inspectors hope to be able to finish out their career in some administrative capacity, preferably as an inspector in charge of a division.

After twelve years of investigating internal theft, during which the responsibility was great; the hours irregular, long, and frequently over weekends and holidays, I was ready for a more normal way of life. In 1961, Roger F. Howe, the assistant inspector in charge at Seattle, announced he would retire. I wrote to Postmaster General J. Edward Day, asking to be considered for the vacancy.

Mr. Howe's decision to retire came during a period of change that follows when the political party in power changes. John F. Kennedy had been elected, and so we had a new administration. I was not alone in the quest for promotion. I knew of at least six of my close contemporaries, each one equally as capable as I, who were all after a promotion at that particular time to Mr. Howe's job or anything else that might come up for grabs. All the big promotions that had come during the Eisenhower years when the fifteen administrative regions were being formed had, of course, gone to Republicans. "Career development" for Democrats during those years was rare, and it had been a long eight years.

People involved in this kind of job selection usually do not discuss what transpires. The name of the game is politics, but politics is not the only consideration. People who make appointments naturally feel and hope they are selecting someone who is qualified and who can adequately handle the particular job for which he is chosen.

Of course, those who achieve advancement usually are recommended by what some call a "rabbi." In this case I was fortunate in having more than one rabbi. It is no secret that both James K. Langan and Reuben Kremers, national officers in the National

Association of Letter Carriers, were among those who were active in my support. Others are not forgotten, but they would probably prefer that their names not be mentioned.

Circumstances also contributed to any advancement. The time was ripe; I had had sufficient experience in criminal investigation which the chief inspector, Henry B. Montague, considered important; and I was known to be of the right political party at the right time but not active in politics. Then a vacancy occurred that I had not particularly anticipated. The inspector in charge, Virgil F. Worthington, elected to step down and take the vacancy created by Mr. Howe's retirement. The chief inspector called me to Washington and, after a long interview, asked me if I would like the position of inspector in charge. A few days later I was promoted to inspector in charge of the five-state Seattle Division, effective March 3, 1962—a position I held until I voluntarily retired December 31, 1966.

Soon after my promotion, Postmaster General J. Edward Day came to Seattle for ceremonies incident to the issuance of a commemorative stamp honoring Seattle's Century Twenty-one World's Fair. I met him and Tyler Abell in the Olympic Hotel the morning of the day the stamp was to be officially issued.

Day was not in a good mood. As far as I could tell, one of the first things he did that morning was read the local newspaper. He was evidently not pleased with the lack of coverage they had given his arrival in town. He probably was hurt that a member of the president's cabinet was given no more than routine coverage.

Sen. Warren G. Magnuson stayed at the Olympic Hotel when he was in Seattle, and he was to accompany Day to the fairground for the ceremony. It had been previously planned that Day would hand the senator the first letter delivered through the station. This letter was to have been a congratulatory letter from President Kennedy to Senator Magnuson. Through some oversight, no such letter had ever been prepared.

When he found this out, J. Edward Day was furious, and said to Tyler Abell, "I hate gimmicks because they aren't true! You figure out something."

It wasn't necessary. Senator Magnuson rose to the occasion. He took a blank letterhead, enclosed it in one of his own printed envelopes, and had one of the new commemorative stamps stuck on it. The plan was reversed; the letter was addressed to the president and was to be the first one mailed at the new Space Needle post office station. This was a much better plan anyway. After the ribbon was cut and the press had its pictures of the senator and postmaster general mailing the letter, the postmaster general's mood improved. We escorted him through the World's Fair exhibits.

President Kennedy never did receive that first letter mailed with the Century Twenty-One World's Fair commemorative stamp. The envelope with the blank piece of paper was intercepted and given to the postmaster general. He probably kept it as a personal commemorative of one day in the public life of a boss mailman.

One of the better-known postmaster generals was James J. Farley, who held the position for almost eight years (March 1933 to September 1940). He was well known for his wide acquaintanceship with politicians and postal employees. It was said he never forgot a name. Farley, a very political animal, developed an ability to remember names. Of course, he had to have help.

One time when he visited Denver, his advance man obtained the names of everyone the "general" might run into on his trip. His first stop when he entered the Denver post office was at the blind man's stand. He made a small purchase and called the man by his first name, asking how he was getting along. This went on throughout the building, and he seemed to have no trouble remembering people's names. If you doubt that people greeted in this way by a prominent official are not impressed, you are mistaken.

Another political type was W. Don Brewer. His career was a political classic. Brewer was appointed postal inspector from a rural route in Kentucky. He was assigned to the Seattle Division and was soon sent on an audit trip throughout Alaska.

While he was in Anchorage, he was invited to address a service club. His speech was called "Let Me Set You Straight." The talk was strongly criticized on the front page of Atwood's *Anchorage Times* that same evening. Atwood had attended the meeting and didn't like what he heard. Brewer had said that Alaskans, and particularly Alaskan postmasters, set themselves above the rules and regulations governing other U.S. citizens. He said they seemed to feel that they were entitled to special privileges because of their remote geographical location. Alaskans failed to appreciate this kind of service-club preaching.

Publicity of this nature, when it filters to the seat of our federal government, creates flack. Politicians in Washington, D.C., of either political party, do not like bad publicity. Explanations for the talk were demanded by Brewer's Inspector in Charge Melvin Northrip, Chief Postal Inspector Clifton C. Garner, and probably Postmaster General Jesse M. Donaldson. Postal inspectors were expected to be silent investigators, not public speakers or politicians.

Brewer soon left the Seattle Division, no doubt sensing he was in a cul-de-sac after this experience.

However, when the Republican party again regained power under Eisenhower, Brewer's political lamp was relit and he was soon named regional director for the five-state Denver Post Office Region. He was a verbose individual and a good speaker. He had learned to tailor his talks to adhere to the party line and knew what the public wanted to hear. Now he was expected to talk at many functions.

Brewer's star again reached a nadir when John F. Kennedy was elected president. He was soon edged out as regional director in Denver. The job was a supergrade and so he was not protected by civil service. I met him next in the lobby of the Continental Hotel in Washington when I was in the capital in 1963 for a conference of inspectors in charge.

"They have asked me to head up the O.K. Rubber Welders," Brewer announced. This firm was a national tire recapping concern.

Under Brewer's leadership the company, which had been losing money, prospered. The stock was selling at $3.00 a share when he took over and when the firm was sold to Ashland Oil three years later in 1966, the stock brought $18.40. After this, Brewer took a year's leave of absence from the company to join Maurice H. Stans in New York for the Nixon campaign. During the campaign, twenty-nine million dollars was raised, far more than had ever before been raised in any political campaign.

Then the wheel of fortune again turned for Brewer. He was fifty-six when Nixon was elected president and the Republicans regained power. When I saw Brewer a short time after the election, he proudly said, "Maury has given me a top commerce job covering four states."

"Maury" was Maurice H. Stans, Nixon's new secretary of commerce. Stans had been deputy postmaster general under Eisenhower from October 1955 until 1957. Stans later became deeply involved in the Committee to Reelect the President (Nixon).

The top job Brewer referred to was federal cochairman of the Commerce Department's Four Corners Regional Commission involved in economic development of distressed areas in Colorado, New Mexico, Utah, and Arizona.

A few months after this, President Nixon asked Brewer to take over as deputy administrator for the Small-Business Administration. Then in 1970 he was appointed for a seven-year term as commissioner of the Interstate Commerce Commission. He stayed with the ICC until 1973, when he retired and returned to Denver.

Brewer certainly had a good and faithful rabbi in Maurice H. Stans. There was one thing about Brewer: he never changed politics, as so many do when they feel it might help them obtain a promotion or some patronage job. Brewer recently passed away while living in retirement in Denver.

Leading the host of people telling us what we can or cannot do today are the federal, state, and district court judges. Judges are usually appointed through politics, although they may be recommended by their bar associations. This selection process naturally produces many judges who are really incompetent. A few seem to have a knack of getting into areas they should leave to the legislative arm of our government. We do seem to acquire a majority of fair, responsible, and capable judges, which is fortunate because their power has become tremendous.

During my law enforcement years, it was part of my business to talk to many who had been charged with federal crimes. Those awaiting sentencing in the Western District of Washington were always hopeful that they could have their case assigned to some judge other than Judge George Boldt. The jail-house lawyers would warn them that they would "get a jolt from Boldt."

One judge in the Western District of Washington who for many years heard most of the postal and Secret Service cases was Judge John Bowen. He frequently made it clear that he felt all law enforcement people really didn't have the respect they should for him and the court. He also believed it was his obligation to aid in the training of all young United States attorneys. He would frequently instruct and criticize them in open court. I believe most of them feared him, except John Dore, who frequently simply ignored the judge's requests.

Judge Bowen would rarely openly berate a law enforcement officer from the bench. He would send them notes delivered by his bailiff. He once sent a note to an experienced Secret Service agent, asking him to pull up his socks. He once sent me a note suggesting I be more attentive during one of his long, dry, monotonous charges to the jury. Special agents of the FBI were not above receiving notes from the judge. Their socks were not always pulled up or their attire otherwise pleasing to his honor. They might even be whispering to someone nearby, and that disturbed him.

The judge had some strong feelings that sometimes influenced his thinking. We had a case where a young man in his thirties was convicted of stealing mail from house letter boxes to obtain checks, which he managed to cash. He was married, had two children, and was out of work.

When he came before the judge for sentencing, the probation officer made a favorable report. After a fatherly talk to the defendant, the judge told him he would defer sentencing for six months, to allow him to obtain gainful employment. He was released and ordered to reappear in six months.

After the allotted time, the man returned to court. The judge asked him if he had a steady job, and he seemed pleased when the man proudly reported that he was working and supporting his wife and children. Then the roof fell in!

"What do you do?" asked the judge.

"I took some training and was able to get a job at the Woodland Park Zoo," answered the man.

"Am I to understand that you work in a place where they keep animals caged?" queried the judge.

"Yes."

After lecturing the man on his horrible choice of work, he summarily sentenced him to nine months in prison. The unfortunate defendant had no chance to explain that there is more to taking care of animals than scooping up the dung. Lions have headaches, elephants have tender feet, and other animals have ailments that must be continuously attended to. The judge seemed to conclude that the young man actually enjoyed seeing animals locked up. Evidently the judge had strong feelings about zoos.

Fortunately misuse of power by judges is not common. The responsibility that goes with the job must be safeguarded, and no judge should sit on the bench after reaching age seventy. Most attorneys and judges are opposed to early retirement, but they are not the ones who come before the courts for rulings and sentencing.

In 1966 it was decided that a postal code of ethics should be adopted to assure that no postal employee would have any conflict of interest. Naturally, very few of the rank-and-file postal employees could conceivably have a conflict of interest. The code of ethics was directed to the administrative people, which then amounted to an unbelievable 9 percent of the force.

When the code of ethics was enacted into law, there were penalty clauses for violations. Historically, it would be the job of inspectors to investigate suspected violations and then to present the evidence to the Department of Justice for prosecution.

The general counsel for the Post Office Department at the time was Timothy J. May. In the infinite wisdom of legal anticipation, he evidently decided that it would be embarrassing if some administrative official who was guilty of a serious and deliberate conflict of interest should be prosecuted. Realizing that postal inspectors investigate violations of law, May set up area conferences that were attended by both the inspector in charge and his assistant from each division.

These conferences were ostensibly to discuss and make clear the salient features of the new ethical conduct guidelines. This was, of course, an unnecessary expense, since the law was clearly written. It was obvious that the real purpose of the meeting was to enable May to verbally direct the postal inspectors *not* to present conflict of interest violations to U. S. attorneys for prosecution, unless the case had been reviewed by the general counsel and approval had been obtained. It was also obvious that neither May nor anyone in the general counsel's office dared to issue such instructions in writing, for to do so would be indicative of a cover-up.

This meant that the Post Office Department did not want any postal inspector presenting an ethics case involving an official, such as a regional director, his deputies, or another high official.

Whenever there is an administration change, several bureaucrats in high places either resign, get fired, or attempt to get demoted to some permanent civil service job below what are called the supergrades. Some who are particularly adroit or have their own crystal ball, play it safe.

According to the National Association of Postal Supervisors, just before the fall elections in 1968, the young regional director of the five-state Northwest Region arranged to have himself appointed to the position of postmaster of Seattle, Washington. This was a reduction of about three thousand dollars in his annual salary, but he would have the security of a career employee in the new job.

Being politically astute, he worked it smoother and better than most. He was nominated for the position of postmaster on August 16, 1968, well before the national election, and he had the job nailed down. He did not, however, take it immediately. He waited until after the election to decide. If the Democrats had stayed in, he probably would have given up the appointment and remained regional director, where he administered postal activities for nearly seventeen thousand employees and eighteen hundred post offices.

The Democrats lost, and he accepted the appointment as postmaster for Seattle.

Don Ledbetter, when he was secretary of the National Association of Postal Supervisors commented in his column in the supervisors' magazine that this was not a move of real dedication; it was a move of self-preservation. He said "Like a cat with nine lives, he was also given additional duties of Advisor to the Regional Director, which carried a one-level, one thousand dollar increase."

Consequently, the net result of his smart political maneuver was civil-service protection of his job with only a two-thousand-dollar drop in salary.

For some strange reason, people dislike to pay traffic or parking tickets. They will go to considerable trouble to have a parking ticket fixed and think nothing of asking others to help them in an effort to circumvent the law they have broken.

Those in high offices are not above trying to get cases fixed. While I was inspector in charge, I was once asked by a regional director to kill a case one of our young postal inspectors had been working on.

It was not a big case, as cases go, but it was probably very big to the young inspector because it was his first. He was investigating a case involving a letter carrier in Butte, Montana, who had embezzled funds given him to purchase a uniform. To understand the case better, it should be mentioned that the Butte post office was a very political post office. Even the clerks and letter carriers seemed to think the post office was run by Sen. Mike Mansfield and Rep. Arnold Olsen instead of by the local postmaster. Maybe it was.

"I have just had a call from the senate majority leader (Mike Mansfield), who asked me to have the Butte case killed," the regional director said to me. This was the only time I ever knew of any postal official attempting to interfere with an investigation, although I can imagine there have been many such cases.

I have never believed that Mike Mansfield personally called the regional director and asked him to have the case killed. I have always suspected it was one of those in the senator's office who frequently take independent action in a senator's name without the senator knowing about it. Actually, such an attempt constitutes obstruction of justice, a criminal offense.

To have killed any case would have destroyed everything I felt was right about the work of postal inspectors. It would have seriously damaged the young inspector's respect for his job, and it would have meant I would be abdicating my authority from then on. I refused to kill the case, which certainly did not please the regional director. He threatened to take the matter all the way to the top!

"What am I going to tell the majority leader?" he asked when he realized I was dead serious.

"Tell him that he took the same oath of office I took when we took our jobs, an oath to uphold the laws of the United States."

I never heard any more about killing a case.

One of the tried and true ways to obtain a nice promotion within the postal service is to become president of the National Association of Postmasters of the United States, commonly called NAPUS. Their presidents serve one year and have an office in Washington, D.C. After that year, they supposedly return to their respective post offices and resume work there. It doesn't work that way. The Post Office Department learned long ago that the best way to handle these people was to give their outgoing presidents a juicy administrative job. As a result, the department has very little trouble from the presidents of NAPUS.

During the time I was inspector in charge and kept up with such things, NAPUS presidents John Snyder, Charles Puskar, and James O. Toole either accepted high-level positions in the Post Office Department labyrinth when their one-year terms as president of NAPUS were over or remained in Washington. After his year as NAPUS president, David Trevithick, who was an intellectual, refused a high-paying department job and went back to being postmaster at Salt Lake City.

There are two national organizations of postmasters: NAPUS and the National League of Postmasters. It was also usual for past presidents of the league to accept high-level positions. This is a common malady known widely as "Potomac Fever." When an honest man contracts Potomac Fever, does he truly represent the people who have elected him?

By comparison, no president of the National Association of Letter Carriers, usually called NALC, ever sacrificed the confidence of the letter carriers by accepting a high-paying position in the postal administration. Consequently, they are able to effectively represent the men who elect them. I have known the three that guided the NALC for a fifty-year period ending in 1977. I would have been astounded if any one of them ever thought of accepting a high-paying administration position in the postal service. They were all earnestly and assiduously working full time to represent the letter carriers. Past presidents of the NALC Edward J. Gainor, Bill Doherty, and James H. Rademacher successfully built the letter carriers' association into one of the most powerful labor unions in the country.

10

Purloined Letters

"ON WEDNESDAY MORNING, Arthur Baily, a native of Devonshire, and in the 38th year of his life, was executed near Ilcester, persuant to the sentence for stealing a letter from the Bath Post Office" was the lead story in the Bath, England, *Herald* of September 14, 1811. The article continued:

> He was taken out of prison a little after eight o'clock in the morning, and placed in a cart, attended by Mr. Miller, the under Sheriff, and the Chaplain of the prison in a chaise. He shewed the greatest firmness on the way to the Fatal Tree; and when under the gallows, he joined fervently in prayer, and addressed the spectators audibly. . . . 'Be sure to be honest, and not covet money, cursed money, and particularly money that is not your own.' He was then deprived of his mortal state of existence, dying without a struggle.

This short newspaper report of 1811 surely covered the who, what, when, and where as a good newspaper article should, but the article was silent on the why. Why did poor Arthur steal a letter? How did Arthur know it contained money? Did he break into the post office at night, or did he demand the letter at gunpoint? Perhaps he worked in the post office distributing mail and came across the letter as he worked, noted that it might contain money, then pocketed it.

We will probably never know the details about why Arthur got himself into such a hapless position. From the newspaper report it is obvious the English didn't think much of anyone who stole their mail. But did they? A few short years before, the Colonists in America had fought a war because the King's postmen were opening and reading their mail and nothing at all was being done about it. But let an Arthur Baily steal one letter, and very shortly there was no more Arthur.

It appeared that England had a double standard of justice, but it should be remembered that the Colonists were felt to be revolutionaries. The English, in their national interest, thought it best to keep an eye on them. They opened their mail in connection with their counterespionage concerns.

When the Revolutionary War was won, our country was very concerned about the sanctity of mail. There was a hanging penalty for mail theft from 1792 until 1799, when the penalty was reduced to flogging. Today the penalty for theft or opening of mail is not more than five years of imprisonment.

It would be hard for me to remember the number of times during the 1960s that I proudly addressed service clubs, postal-employee organizations, and other groups, assuring them that the sanctity of the seal on first-class mail was inviolate. It was guaranteed by the Bill of Rights. The Fourth Amendment reads in part: "The right of people to be secure in their persons, houses, papers and effects, against unreasonable searches and seizures shall not be violated."

Even when I was sincerely making such public pronouncements, the FBI and CIA, with the help of postal employees, were busy opening and reading first-class mail. This much they have admitted. The motive was "solely to carry out FBI counterintelligence responsibilities in order to thwart espionage efforts directed against the United States by foreign powers," according to an FBI admission.

Opening of domestic mail without a warrant, by anyone— including an agency of the government—is clearly against the law. Just how much or what kind of mail was opened in the interest of national security during the 1960s is really unknown. Mail going to or from known subversives and spies was removed from the mail stream, turned over to the FBI for "observation," then returned within a few hours. Ten years later, postal inspectors who had knowledge of this surveillance were called to testify before a congressional committee. Not having had any knowledge of this effort, I was never called upon to testify, but I was nevertheless questioned to ascertain if I had known about it.

Just as England had done before 1776, our country felt in the 1960s that it was in the national interest to open certain mail. What has usually not been brought out is the fact that most of the mail opened was mail coming from or going to Soviet Bloc nations. This mail was not legally under the custody of the Post Office Department until it had cleared customs.

Today mail going to certain persons in foreign countries is opened by those countries before it is cleared for delivery. I believe most letters written to a person in an Iron Curtain country will go through that country's mail surveillance system. But they can feel fairly secure in believing that their mail will go through intact without question, for delivery in our country. We are either a very naive nation or else stupid regarding this arrangement.

In 1963, when I was inspector in charge of the Seattle Division, I received a teletype message from Washington asking who had set up what was called the Foreign Propaganda Unit at Seattle, a port of foreign mail exchange. This unit had been quietly set up, and very few, including me, knew of its existence.

As it developed, Washington should have known who had set it up. The unit was set up under law by the Bureau of Customs and the general counsel for the Post Office Department. Representatives of these two agencies quietly visited Seattle and other foreign exchange post offices for that purpose.

The unit was set up to observe all incoming mail from certain countries and to determine what part was propaganda. The bulk of such mail was periodicals and newspapers. When it was propaganda, a card was mailed to the addressee, asking whether or not they wanted such mail sent on to them. When they replied, a file was prepared and placed in a locked container. If the person wanted such mail, it would automatically be sent on to them. If not, it was destroyed.

Some people didn't like receiving such inquiries, particularly educators in our higher institutions of learning. The thing that had Washington in a stir were complaints that the FBI was being furnished information obtained from the Foreign Propaganda Units.

The unit was operated by customs employees, and the file cards were made out and kept by postal employees to enable them to know whether to send the mail along or to destroy it.

We found that an FBI agent regularly visited the unit in Seattle to obtain the names of those who wished to receive foreign propaganda material. An FBI agent had been allowed access to the records by postal supervisors who felt they were acting in the best interests of our country. Of course, no one other than postal employees is permitted access to workroom floors of post offices.

I had to request that the FBI be denied access to the unit. A few days later an FBI agent visited my office and asked why the FBI was being denied access to information records that could be vital to the security of the United States. This was a difficult question for me to answer, but the courts had no trouble; they declared the Foreign Propaganda Unit to be an unconstitutional operation, and so it was closed.

The constant stream of riches that flows through the post office pipeline is staggering. Literally trillions of dollars' worth of money, negotiable securities, and goods pass through the mails. Everything from mink coats to guns, money orders to government checks, diamonds to bank deposits, and credit cards to currency are handled in the daily routine.

It would be hard to arrange a more tempting array of choice riches to set before a weak person. Fortunately, the vast majority of postal employees are totally unconcerned with the contents of the ninety-odd billion pieces of mail they handle each year.

Naturally, greed does tempt a few. However, less than two-tenths of 1 percent of the six hundred thousand postal employees succumb to temptation. Postal inspectors feel that even one depredator is one too many. It is often amazing how much trouble even one can cause in our trusting society.

Generally, the postmaster is the first to hear the bad news. Inspectors swing into action when a postmaster calls and says, "My patrons are raising Ned; they keep losing valuable letters and they are blaming me!"

When this happens, the inspector knows he has to catch the thief and catch him with the goods, or else! He cannot leave a case like this until it is solved. Internal theft is one of the basic reasons for his job. There is no lining up of three hundred or so employees in a mail-handling unit and talking to them or even searching them. To do so would be casting suspicion on 299 dedicated, honest, and loyal employees, while the guilty one might still be free to continue his thefts. Fortunately, inspectors have long had the reputation of unerringly seeking out the guilty.

To catch a thief, a point from which the suspected area can be observed is necessary. Inspectors have secreted themselves in many confining places and in uncomfortable positions in order to observe the actual embezzlement in the fraction of a second it can occur. Inspectors William Earle and R. C. Deyo hid under a staircase behind a false wall panel that had been hastily built for the purpose. Inspector R. F. Howe once secreted himself in the hot attic above the post office, where he laid on planks peering through a small hole he had drilled in the ceiling. Inspector Ralph Smith once crouched in a crate on a Mississippi dock. Others have used panel trucks, periscopes, cardboard boxes, and any blind that would provide them with some cover in order to observe but not to be observed.

Many times the cases were blown; but strangely enough, in a few months the same depredator could not resist the temptation and resumed his peculation. So-called stool pigeons, or informants, are far too unreliable to be used in most internal mail-theft cases. The inspector cannot afford to be wrong when he apprehends an employee, and reliance on others is too dangerous, except in rare cases when no other solution is possible.

To provide the public with security in its mail and to lend a visual deterrent to those who may be tempted, theft-preventive lookouts, or observation galleries, have been installed in about one-tenth of the mail-handling workrooms in the country. The post office building in Philadelphia had lookouts as far back as 1875. One in Richmond, Virginia, dates back to the Civil War.

No other effective deterrent to internal theft has been perfected. Scanning closed television has been tried but without too much success. These galleries are not secret, and, when hired, each employee is told about them and their purpose. They are in plain sight for all to see. They are never used for any purpose other than to observe depredations on mail. Any inspector who might use them to report loitering is immediately subject to disciplinary action. Of course, the galleries are not used unless there are complaints of lost mail. They are not pleasant places for inspectors to loiter, and as a result they stand mostly as a deterrent to theft. The employee, however, never knows exactly when the lookout may be manned, but honest employees soon forget they exist.

In a congressional hearing held in 1965 about observation galleries, the postmaster general stated, "During my extensive travels throughout the nation, no postal worker has ever complained to me about these lookouts."

He should have known that the National Association of Letter Carriers has been complaining about lookout galleries for many years. This is despite the fact that letter carriers are out on the street delivering mail and are inside post offices for only a short period of their workday.

Even with the lookouts, it is not a simple matter to pick out a thief from among a crew of sometimes hundreds of busy workers. To detect the one guilty employee who is able to secret a single letter in a split second often takes days, weeks, and sometimes longer.

For over twelve years, my assignment was to investigate internal mail theft throughout a four-state area. Two inspectors or more are usually assigned to these cases, and during that twelve-year period, I assisted in the apprehension of over one hundred employees. With observations made possible by the lookouts, the guilty employee could be stopped when he left the building with the evidence, thus avoiding embarrassment to any honest worker.

A study made in 1964 disclosed that there were fewer mail-theft cases in those post offices that had observation galleries. When a career registry clerk was arrested by Inspector C. A. Hoyer in Seattle for currency thefts totaling five thousand dollars, he had this to say, "If you fellows had had those lookouts in the vault, I never would have started doing this."

By the year 1965, because of excessive shoplifting and employee theft in supermarkets and merchandising stores, builders began equipping them with observation galleries. The lookouts in retail stores are often manned by off-duty or retired police officers. Nevada gambling casinos have extensive lookout galleries built in above the tables.

The U. S. Postal Service has an obligation to be sure the mail of the public is given as much, or more, protection than that given to a gambler's dollar or a merchant's fur coat.

There is something about a coin that creates a strong attraction for man. When coins are mailed by coin dealers whose mailing labels literally shout that the parcel contains rare and exotic pieces of silver or gold, some impressionable post office employees contract a virus of dishonesty.

Similarly, when the U. S. Mint mails proof sets to numismatists, there are those who suddenly develop a desire to become coin collectors.

Postal inspectors are well aware that dishonesty is contagious, and if one gets away with a theft, it will make it easier for others to succumb to temptation. Certain steps can be taken to prevent internal theft, but it is a battle that never ends, and no quarter is given. If a thief is caught, he will be arrested and prosecuted; every postal employee knows this. Nevertheless, occasions do arise that defy both preventive safeguards and the threat of punitive action.

One example of a situation that was difficult to stifle began in 1964 when inspectors were plagued with a coin-loss epidemic that snowballed, and its course wasn't stayed until 1966. Before it was over, more than 150 employees nationwide had been apprehended for embezzling coin shipments.

In 1964 the Philadelphia Mint mailed almost four million proof sets to numismatists. Almost from the first mailing, complaints of loss were made. Postal inspectors were shocked by 38,169 complaints of lost coin shipments.

Most of the mint mailings were sent by unnumbered, insured, parcel post. The next year the U. S. assay office in San Francisco began mailing special mint sets. This time the postal and treasury departments got together, and the coins were sent by registered mail. With continual surveillance and occasional arrests, the losses decreased each year until only one parcel was lost in 1967.

Coin collectors also buy coins from dealers who conduct a mail-order business. One such firm was the W. H. Foster Co. of Walla Walla. Hercules C. Picerne was president, and Robert A. Naimy was vice-president, of the firm, which was later called Hercaimy Enterprises.

Again in 1964, coin shipments made by the Walla Walla coin dealer seemed to be a prime target for mail depredators. Total losses of this firm and others in the Northwest amounted to 585, which had a combined value of $23,380.66, a staggering sum and a situation that demanded attention.

The investigation began at Walla Walla, where the workroom of the post office could easily be observed from observation galleries. It required only a short time to determine that the mailings were actually being made (which is not always the case in such situations), and that no one in Walla Walla was taking the parcels.

In the meantime, a concerned R. A. Naimy was busy writing letters to Sen. Warren G. Magnuson and Rep. Catherine May about the mail losses of the company's coins. Naimy also sent a telegram to the president of the United States and corresponded frequently with the Post Office Department in Washington D. C.

Postal Inspector Leo J. Peterson had been assigned the case, but a great many other postal inspectors worked on it. By the end of 1965, it had become evident that most of the losses were occurring in the Chicago post office, where distribution was made for the eastern part of the country, a long way from Walla Walla.

Naimy, still writing to Senator Magnuson, stated in a letter to him: "A fine postal inspector has been assigned to our case. He has less chance of cleaning up the Chicago P. O. alone than Buz Sawyer (of the comics) taking on the entire Russian Navy.'' Naimy also commented to the senator that the thefts had stopped for nearly five weeks but started again with alarming vigor.

Concentrated investigation had been underway at Chicago by this time, but the mail-handling area there was immense, employing hundreds of people. Special lookouts had to be improvised.

After four months of concentrated attention, the inspectors had enough evidence to arrest two employees. They found that one of the two would throw sacks of mail from Walla Walla off a moving belt to another employee, who would open them, take out the coin shipments, cut them open with a knife, and remove the coins. The empty coin wrappings were discarded wherever it was convenient, generally into mail sacks going to a variety of cities. The two had prepared a blind behind loaded mail dollys where they could cut open the coin parcels out of sight of the observation galleries they knew might be manned by postal inspectors.

When the two were arrested, the losses stopped. Naimy stopped writing to Congress, and we stopped getting correspondence on congressional stationery.

People are bound to react in many unexpected ways when suddenly confronted by a major crisis, and being arrested for a theft of mail presents a very sudden shift in a person's normal life-style. Although I have been in jails and in the penitentiary many times, I was there on business and never experienced the feeling of having the iron door slammed behind me.

At one time in Seattle we were working on a case involving three young women who had been taking letters out of street letter boxes, then cashing the checks they found in the mail. In due course we were able to identify the girls and learned where they lived. Their small apartment was located on the second floor of an old house in the skid-row area. When the evidence was complete, we went up to their room one morning early, accompanied by a police matron because we were dealing with women.

Two of the girls were still in bed, and while the matron went in to tell them they were under arrest and to get them up and dressed, I remained in the adjoining kitchen with a young Navy man who just happened to be visiting them. He was obviously emotionally upset by the intrusion and felt a need to protect the girls. He pulled a knife and, without saying a word, began to advance toward me.

"Don't you think you had better give me that knife, son?" I heard myself saying.

The young sailor paused a second, then handed the knife over to me, handle first. These things happen quickly, and I don't know what I would have done if he hadn't changed his mind.

Another case involved Norman Pepperling, who lived in the O. K. Hotel in Seattle, which offered rooms at very low rates. Pepperling, out of money, snatched the purse of a woman who was walking alone, then beat her. She was treated for brain concussion and facial cuts. Pepperling was arrested by the Seattle police and confined in the city jail.

The man was a logger by profession, but he had worked the previous Christmas at the post office as a temporary employee. While he was working in the post office, he stole a letter that contained a sixty-five-dollar check, which he cashed at a local sporting goods store. I went down to the city jail to talk to him about the mail theft.

One of the city detectives brought him to the fifth floor, and we sat down to talk. The detective had other work to do and so left us alone in the room. I was sitting with my back to the window, and he was sitting adjacent to me. It was a large room where detectives did their paperwork when they were not out on the street.

This man, who was only twenty-nine, talked freely and calmly about taking the check and cashing it. He wrote out his own admission, and when he had signed it, he said, "I've always wanted to commit suicide." He jumped up and ran for the small window behind me, which he struck with his shoulder, then plummeted through. In the instant this happened, I had managed to grab him around the waist, but his momentum carried him through, dragging my wrist through the broken glass. He was gone, dropping five stories to the street below. Although he was immediately taken to the hospital, he died three hours later. When the man fell, his body barely missed the U. S. commissioner who was just entering the building.

Occurrences like this attract people instantly, including reporters who demand to know what happened. It was the same day Gen. Douglas MacArthur arrived in San Francisco after being relieved of his Far East assignment by President Truman. Luckily for me, most of the news that day was devoted to the general.

The most difficult part was trying to explain to the man's family what had happened. They, of course, suspected police brutality. The jumper had a previous long record of mental disorder unknown at the time to either the police or me. He had been in an Oregon mental institution and had only recently been released from the Veteran's mental hospital at American Lake, Washington.

In another internal mail-theft case, we had caught an elderly man who had been taking small items from the mail while he was working as a Christmas extra. The case didn't seem too serious to us, but apparently it was to him.

We talked to him, obtained his address, which was a room in a cheap hotel nearby, then released him and asked that he come to the postal inspector's office the next morning at nine. There seemed no reason to put the man in jail, because he obviously wasn't a person who had ever been locked up and the crime didn't warrant it.

The following morning we waited for him to appear, but by ten o'clock he had still not shown up. Thinking that he had perhaps skipped, we went down to his hotel. The room clerk told us the man hadn't come down, and the clerk went with us up to the room.

We found our elderly mail thief in bed sound asleep. An empty box of sleeping tablets was on the night table with a suicide note to his family back East. It was a close call. The police ambulance took him to the hospital, where he was revived. In his mind, he had committed a very serious crime and was too embarrassed to face life. The United States attorney decided not to prosecute, stating he felt the man had suffered enough. The stolen mail was sent along to the addressee.

We had another case where a respected citizen lost a great deal more than a few years behind bars. For his sake, we will call him Mickey. After Inspector Mark Blake and I had picked him up for stealing mail, he said, "I have just lost the two most important things in my life—my postal career and my military career!"

We had stopped Mickey one evening a few yards from the post office employee door after he left the building when his tour was over. Mickey had seven first-class letters concealed inside his shirt, all addressed to charitable and religious organizations, and all appeared to contain cash.

Why did we pick on Mickey when there was a score of other postal clerks who handled, and could have stolen, the same mail? The letters were addressed to the Red Cross, March of Dimes, Union Gospel Mission, Youth for Christ, and the Marcus Whitman Foundation.

We had spent a great many hours of work before we knew Mickey was actually the one who was taking the mail we had complaints about. The post office where he worked had observation galleries. As careful and as coy and as secretive as Mickey was, he was finally seen from these galleries when he secreted a letter inside his shirt. At last we knew we were on the right track, but we needed to be positive. Postal employees are respected persons, all of whom are considered to be above suspicion. To apprehend the wrong man could bring his reputation into question and would be very embarrassing to both the man and to the inspectors who were wrong.

So we watched Mickey for several hours, let him go home with stolen mail in his shirt, and again watched him a second day before we stopped him as he left the building. Now we were sure.

We really didn't know Mickey from any of the other employees. It turned out that when we apprehended him in 1951 he was back working in the post office after having served his country in World War II. He had seen military duty in the South Pacific, and when arrested he was a lieutenant colonel in the National Guard, a high position of which he was rightfully proud. Mickey was a man who was well respected in his community, had a fine family, owned his own home, and was apparently not in serious need of the few dollars he was taking out of the letters he stole. It is not possible to imagine his thoughts when he threw away two careers and a reputation.

Mickey was not without many friends. His friends, wishing to help Mickey, brought pressure to have him exonerated or at least to have the case dropped. If he was convicted of mail theft, he would no doubt lose his commission as a lieutenant colonel in the guard. Our boss received a letter from a powerful senator in Mickey's behalf.

The United States attorney who was to prosecute the case had Inspector Blake and me travel three hundred miles to meet with him in his office. He exclaimed to us. "This is the hottest case I've ever had. I want to talk it over."

Talk we did, but *we* could not see why the case was so hot. The Constitution was written so that the people of our country would be secure in their papers, including letters containing money. Our job was to assure the sanctity of the seal on first-class mail to all people. The U. S. attorney finally decided to do what he had taken an oath to do, uphold the law.

Certainly not all the mail thefts are committed by postal employees. Mail must be handled by many people along the way, and frequently less-dedicated workmen are tempted by the riches in the mail that pass through their hands. There was one such case I'll never forget.

In January 1959, I arrived in Anchorage on an assignment to assist Inspector Carl A. Hoyer on a series of air force currency shipments that had disappeared. When I arrived at the Anchorage International Airport, I noticed that the waiting room was literally a hall of fame for the pioneer Alaskan bush pilots. On the walls hung portraits of many of those famous men. Later, after the 1964 Good Friday earthquake, the valuable pictures were taken down, but were never rehung there when the building was restored.

Easy cases are soon forgotten, tough ones are remembered; but the unresolved are sometimes seared into memory forever. The case I was to help on we called the Cape Newenhem Caper, and it turned out not to be one of the average successfully investigated cases, although we did apprehend the guilty person.

In several respects the case seemed to parallel the old Black Bear Case of the dogsled days. The amount of money stolen from registered mail, thirty thousand dollars, was the same; the offender eventually went free; but the IRS demanded and received tax on the proceeds of the thefts. However, the Newenhem Caper lacked the entrancing interest of a female codefendant.

The press was interested, of course, and a year after I reached Anchorage, the *Daily Times* commented under a heading entitled "Missing Payrolls," "At least three payrolls totalling more than thirty thousand dollars have vanished within the past two years. The manner in which the payrolls disappeared . . . indicates a phantom thief of the greatest cunning and dexterity is at large in Alaska."

The article went on to report that "certain airline and postal employees got the third degree, but nobody was able to pin anything on them." This made interesting reading but seemed a little wide of the truth because it was written after we had long since arrested the person who was responsible. However, the grand jury had twice failed to return an indictment, which was not too unusual in Alaska, even in those days.

Three different payrolls had been lost, all of which were mailed by the air force finance officer at Elmendorf AFB, Anchorage, to a remote A. C. & W. Squadron at Cape Newenhem on the extreme west coast of Alaska. The one mailed in February 1958 contained over $10,000; another mailed in December, nine months later, contained over $9,000; and the third, mailed January 16, 1959, contained $9,033, all in small denomination bills. Funds for the squadron payroll were mailed each month by registered mail that was carried exclusively by air.

The first loss was belatedly discovered when a delayed pouch arrived at Cape Newenhem with a slit in its side and the currency shipment missing. The original investigation extended from Anchorage to Cape Newenhem, a distance of several hundred miles of ice and snow. All three losses were dispatched from Anchorage on a Fairchild F-27 Propjet as far as Bethel, where they were unloaded. There the pouch would remain until a bush plane would take the mail to Platinum. Again the mail would await another bush plane for its final leg over to Cape Newenhem.

When the first loss was reported, a postal inspector immediately began an investigation. The case was wide open, because the currency could have been slipped out of the slit pouch by almost anyone who could have had a reasonable access to it—postal employee, airline employee, air force personnel, or someone who slipped into any one of the storage areas where mail was held awaiting further dispatch.

Since it was an air force shipment, the Air Force Office of Special Investigations (OSI) assisted in the original investigation. After a few months it began to look as if the theft were a one-shot caper. Then nine months later a second currency shipment disappeared. This time, pouch and all. It helped that the loss was discovered at Platinum when the bush plane arrived from Bethel. This cut down the search distances somewhat.

When the second loss occurred, Postal Inspector Carl A. Hoyer of Seattle, who always seemed to be selected for the toughest cases, was sent north. He had little more to work with, but he did learn that a certain airline employee at Anchorage had handled both shipments. Furthermore, the employee had quit his humdrum job soon after the first loss to enter upon a life of leisure, only to go back to work at his old job just before the second currency shipment disappeared.

It seemed likely the man came across the first currency dispatch by accident when he noticed the slit in a mail pouch. After exploring it further, he was rewarded by finding ten thousand dollars in the parcel. The second time, he probably felt it was better to take the entire pouch, because this time he had to rip it open to be sure the currency shipment was in it.

With this much to go on, Inspector Hoyer asked for help, and I was sent to join him at Anchorage. The next currency shipment to Cape Newenhem was transported under conditions we controlled as much as possible, without the aid of any means to watch what occurred in the Anchorage International Airport Terminal. The currency was all listed, bill by bill. Its preparation and enclosure in the pouch was witnessed. The pouch was accompanied to the airport, where it was turned over to the suspected employee and taken by him into the building.

The next checkpoint was aboard the airplane that carried mail west. It was my job to get aboard the plane as a passenger to avoid any suspicion and as soon as the mail handler had loaded his mail, to search to determine if the pouch had been brought aboard and if it was intact. This turned out to be a more time-consuming job than contemplated, because there were five thousand pounds of mail in the forward part of the F-27, all pretty well thrown in together with freight. Nevertheless, the pouch couldn't be found, but by then the plane had taken off.

The copilot was an old-time pioneer bush pilot I knew, and he sent my coded message for Inspector Hoyer to the president of the airline who was supposed to be standing by. Instead of waiting for the message, the president decided to take a long lunch break about this time. In the meantime, the suspect finished his tour of duty at 1:00 P.M. and left the airport. Inspector Hoyer didn't receive my message until almost 1:30 P.M. The air force OSI personnel, who were to help in the apprehension, suddenly had a conference, and their commanding officer decided they couldn't help because the offender was not on a military base.

This left the lone inspector in Anchorage with that well-known "moment of truth" decision, whether to pick up the suspect immediately or to wait until he had help. He elected to apprehend the suspect because of the large amount of money involved.

The suspect was by this time back at his home. He refused to permit a search of his home or his automobile, and so he was taken to the inspector's office for questioning. There he denied stealing any mail of any kind, anytime. He agreed to take a lie-detector test to prove his innocence, but later he refused to take it and would make no further statements. He called a well-known Anchorage attorney, and then he was remanded to jail.

In the interim, attempts were made to obtain a search warrant so that the suspect's home and automobile could be legally searched.

Delay was caused by the unfamiliarity of the assistant U. S. attorney with search warrants. The next morning the defendant was out of jail on bail long before the search warrant was issued. Needless to say, the ensuing search of his premises was useless, although many items obviously stolen from the mail were noted among his household possessions.

What happened to the currency? Evidence later determined that it was placed in a safe-deposit box he had previously rented after the second currency shipment had been stolen. Legally there was no way for us to gain access to the box. For days we waited outside the bank, ready to pick up the defendant if he should enter his box and come out with any currency. He soon realized this, and, afraid to attempt to take any money out of the box himself, he gave his attorney the power to do so.

When the attorney came to the bank and took out the safe-deposit box and removed material from it, we asked him to show us what he was taking. He, of course, declined to do so; and the assistant U. S. attorney restrained us from making a physical search of the attorney's pockets. This pretty well blew the case! We went before the grand jury twice with good circumstantial evidence, and on both occasions they postponed a decision on the case, awaiting additional evidence.

All things, both good and bad, eventually come to an end, and eventually the statute of limitations had run out. After this we could talk freely to the defendant's attorney. He told us we had the right man and said the currency was taken out of Anchorage to Seattle by the defendant's sister-in-law, concealed in a blanket covering her month-old baby. In Seattle the currency was washed, that is, exchanged for funds that could not be identified.

Strangely, justice did prevail in a way. As in the Black Bear Case, the Internal Revenue Service, in the course of time, collected income tax from the defendant, based on his excessive increase in net worth, which he had not been reporting. The law makes no exception for reportable income, no matter how one goes about getting it.

11

Mail Pickpockets

SCHEMES TO SEPARATE the gullible and greedy from their money, property, or other things, are legion. To avoid direct confrontation, those who promote such schemes frequently use the U. S. Mail. Of course, anytime the mail is used anywhere along the line in the promotion of a fraud, the case becomes a federal offense.

Fraud is usually called white-collar crime. The police usually call it bunco, those who live by it call it skam, and postal inspectors call it mail fraud.

There are so many different schemes to defraud that one rarely needs to be used a second time. Fraud artists are usually congenial, gregarious people who often demonstrate rare genius in the development and execution of new skams.

Floating and selling stocks and bonds has always been a sophisticated way to clip the greedy. One watered-stock swindle happened to a very big and highly respected company.

Between 1938 and 1940, the one-hundred-year-old eighty-six-million dollar McKesson-Robbins Drug Company was taken for over twenty-one million dollars by the four Musica brothers. When the case broke, there was a great deal of public interest, and the reputation of the drug company was severely damaged through no fault of its own.

When the Musica brothers managed to gain control of McKesson-Robbins, Frank Donald Coster was put in as president.

Frank Coster's real name was Phillip Musica. He managed to have his brother, who had taken the name of George Dietrich, put in as executive vice-president; and another brother, known as Robert Dietrich, took charge of shipping at the Fairfield, Connecticut, plant of McKesson-Robbins. A fourth brother, who had taken the name of Arthur Vernard, remained in the background away from the plant.

Having full control, Coster proceeded to enter into rapid expansion of the drug firm. He floated large issues of stock and by questionable means gained the controlling interest in as many as forty-six drugstores in forty-six different states.

He sold one issue of stock amounting to twenty-five million dollars, showing in the prospectus that the company owned gigantic stores of crude drugs, which they actually did not have. These crude drugs were alleged to be in the custody of various suppliers throughout the world. Fictitious assets totalling twenty-one million dollars were claimed.

Eventually, one of the foremost accounting firms in the country conducted an audit and reported satisfaction with the financial standing of the company. They were wrong because the Musicas fooled them, and rather simply too.

After the auditors were told by the Musicas of McKesson-Robbins that the twenty-one million dollars in crude drugs were being held by suppliers all over the world, the accounting firm wrote to the names furnished, asking each what the value of crude drugs being held were worth. Favorable replies were received, accounting for the alleged twenty-one million dollars and the accountants were satisfied.

Meanwhile, the Musica brother known as Arthur Vernard was busy writing letters. He was replying to the accountants' inquiries on fancy printed stationery in the name of the suppliers. He used as many as eight different typewriters and did all this from a small apartment in Brooklyn, New York. He simply posed as the various fictitious suppliers and, after being told by his brother Coster just what to reply, wrote to the accountants reporting on the crude drugs held for McKesson-Robbins.

Vernard's fraudulent use of the mails brought the postal inspectors into the case. After a lengthy investigation, the true facts came to light, and Coster (Phillip Musica) learned that he and his three brothers were to be arrested. He couldn't face the prospect of prison after the affluent, luxurious life he had been living and so committed suicide.

The two-year investigation had turned up the information that Phillip Musica, alias Frank Coster, had been operating fraudulent schemes since 1913. During the prohibition era he had been associated with a gang of bootleggers who were probably responsible for over twenty murders. Finally, Phillip had decided to quit the gang. He turned informer, and his former associates were all jailed.

Needless to say, bootlegging gangs of that era did not take kindly to what was called the double cross. Consequently, as soon as he became head of McKesson-Robbins as Frank Coster, they systematically proceeded to blackmail him.

Trying to keep up with that situation, besides promoting fraudulent stock manipulations, he also went back into bootlegging. He manufactured a hair tonic that was really an alcoholic beverage. He even tried his hand at gunrunning on a big scale to keep abreast of the blackmail demands, but he had to end it all!

Big companies are not the only ones to be ripped off; you could be too.

Are you a bargain hunter? Does your interest quicken when you think you might get something free? If so, you may be a good mark for the well-groomed shyster who will promise you a second income and at the same time guarantee to improve your home. New siding on the house, a new roof, a public-address burglar alarm system, or a central vacuum-cleaning system can be yours with little effort on your part, they will tell you.

Here is the way it is explained. You show your good faith by having the device installed so that you can show it to your friends. You sign a contract which obligates you to pay for the product, but you can receive commissions from every sale to another customer you recommend. The shysters will tell you the commissions will roll in, pay for the product, and enable you to realize a net profit besides.

All you need to do is give them the names of several of your friends, and for each one who buys a similar device, you get a fifty-dollar reduction on your bill. That isn't all; when your friend buys the product, and recommends others, you still get a commission on that sale and so on.

Too good to be true? It is. Once you have signed the contract, your chances of getting anything but a bill for payment are remote.

Many victims have received a card from a friend, telling them what a fine product the friend bought and suggesting they let a salesman talk to them. Without some entry, most people would not permit a salesman to enter their home. Under the chain referral, they hardly realize they are customers.

The story Mrs. Jones told inspectors is typical of cases of this kind. Mrs. Jones said, "A salesman made a date with my husband and me to show us this easy way to buy a central vacuum-cleaning system for one thousand dollars. We really didn't need it; we are elderly and the children are all gone. The salesman promised us we could earn it simply by giving him the names of some of the people we know. We agreed to let him come to the house one evening.

"A nice-looking young man showed up and started right in by asking if we knew how much is paid out for advertising in this country every year. Thirty-four billion dollars, he told us. He went on to explain that his firm had hired a research company to find out how many people visit the average home each year. He said that they came up with the figure of twelve. He suggested we certainly had more visitors than twelve a year in our lovely home.

"The salesman explained that it was their experience that out of all those who are given a chance to get in on the program, at least half take advantage of it. He went on to suggest that we could easily have six that would come in out of all our friends, which should be enough. He explained the program this way:

" 'Say the unit costs you one thousand dollars, but for the six friends who buy, you get fifty dollars each. That's three hundred dollars—a whole year's payment—right there. But that's only a start. Let's say your friends only know twelve people, and let's say only six of those come in. You get $40 for each one of their friends who comes in too, which is six times $40, or $240 each for six friends, or $1,400. Add this to your three hundred, and that's seventeen hundred dollars. You have not only paid for your central vacuum-cleaning system, but you have seven hundred dollars extra.' "

Then the pressure really started, Mrs. Jones reported. It seemed the whole thing had to be done that night when she and her husband were together. The contract was long, and there was a lot of fine print. The salesman kept talking when they tried to read it. She said they asked one question: Wouldn't it be hard to find enough people to buy the units so that everyone could pay for theirs this way? Mrs. Jones said the salesman explained that their friends would know different people, and the same with their friends, etc. Anyway, he had said that they didn't need to worry, that their unit would be paid for by that time. The Joneses signed the contract because it was getting late and they were tired.

The firm the salesman worked for wasn't slow. The system was installed the next day. That's how fast they work. The Joneses were pleased with the whole deal and sent in the names of twenty of their friends. Then Mr. Jones found out that the system would have cost only five hundred dollars if it had been put in by a local businessman.

The Jones family soon received a bill from a finance company who had bought the contract from the people who had installed the vacuum system. Of course they had nothing to do with the sale nor with the promises made, and eventually they threatened to put a lien against the property if payments were not made.

The result was that the Joneses ended up paying one thousand dollars for a five hundred-dollar vacuum-cleaning system they really didn't need in the first place. A few of their friends didn't like being recommended as pigeons to a fast-talking shyster salesman. One of their friends did buy the system, but the Joneses were never able to squeeze even one fifty-dollar commission out of the operators.

Individuals and families are certainly not the only ones who can be bilked. Even the federal government is not above being a mark for some shysters. On one occasion two enterprising young men

174

who were doing time in the penitentiary selected the Internal Revenue Service as a likely mark.

It was in the late 1950s, and the two cons were expecting to be released early in the year. They turned to contemplate what they might do when they got out. We'll call one Smokey and the other Kiter.

Smokey, who had gone up for stealing other peoples' checks out of mailboxes and cashing them, didn't want to try that again. His friend Kiter had fallen for juggling some books and for embezzlement. He didn't think it would be easy for him to get a job as a bookkeeper again. After considering many things, good and bad, they finally hit upon a scheme that would fit in with their respective talents. They decided on a way to get checks without stealing them.

As soon as they were out, they got together to work on their scheme. Kiter, with his knowledge of bookkeeping, laboriously prepared about thirty different income-tax return forms, all figured to show a substantial refund due but still well within reason. Each had to have a different name. Smokey helped by going about the streets of Seattle, taking down the numbers of houses located near different branch post offices. Picking up blank forms was easy, even the necessary W-2 forms, which were prepared under the name of some responsible local firm that employed help. Kiter knew what he was doing, and the returns were well done.

Now, there was no way for them to intercept income-tax refunds coming back to fictitious names at scattered addresses. Their simple solution to this problem was to rent a box at the main post office. They then filed a series of forwarding orders, which served the addresses they had picked, using the names Kiter had entered on the fake returns.

After carefully checking their work, they mailed the income-tax returns to the Internal Revenue Service about the time of the year it seemed the IRS would be most busy. Kiter was betting the IRS would mail out refund checks before anything was suspected.

Like many such schemes, things just didn't work out right through no particular fault of Smokey or Kiter. Early in the game,

175

an alert letter carrier couldn't understand why a government envelope of the type that contains refund checks came for a name he had never heard of to the address of one of his patrons. He did have a forwarding order for the person, but, being curious, he asked the people on his route if the letter was for some friend or relative. They had never heard of the name either.

The rest was not easy, but it started a chain of events that sent Smokey and Kiter right back to McNeil Island to spend some more time. The letter carrier told his foreman, and the foreman called the postal inspector. They called the Internal Revenue Service, and both began checking. At first, no one knew how many checks had been issued, who they were made out to, or where they were sent.

Obviously the first thing to do was to watch the box at the main post office and to talk to anyone who picked up the mail. For days no one did. In the meantime the checking went on. Out of thirty fictitious names, we soon came up with a couple of real ones, Smokey and Kiter.

Smokey wasn't too hard to find. He had taken a job painting and was found on a ladder painting a house. At first he denied any part of such a "wild idea," but he had already cashed one of the refund checks, and his handwriting gave him away. Then he admitted the caper, not without some pride in his part in the scheme.

Kiter had gone to Arizona, leaving Smokey to "take the heat," but Arizona was not far enough. He was located shortly and brought back. The IRS people no doubt tightened things up so that schemes of this kind could be detected sooner than they were in the 1950s, but they would surely have gotten around to it in time anyway.

Did Smokey and Kiter learn their lesson? We heard that after Kiter got out the second time, he went to work for a nationally known income-tax service. He should be good at it.

Most of us have enough trouble with one income-tax return, let alone thirty.

In these days of fast communications and air travel, the fast-buck boys don't have to limit themselves to any one country. The world is theirs for the taking! To combat international crime, the two best-known crime fighters are Interpol—an international police agency—and the International Association of the Chiefs of Police.

Among crime fighters, there is always a pride in one's own organization, but for the most part law enforcement people around the world have a cohesive understanding, and their mutual cooperation is forged by the very nature of their work. One such case where many law enforcement people worked together was the big bank rip-off in 1964.

There never seems to be an end to new schemes dreamed up to turn a dishonest buck. For a while, a group of enterprising South Americans worked a nefarious scheme on U. S. banks that netted them about four hundred thousand dollars in a few weeks.

It began January 24, 1964, when a New York bank received a letter from one of its depositors who lived in Brazil. The letter was postmarked Zurich, Switzerland, and the depositor asked that ninety-five hundred dollars be sent to a new account he had opened in a Zurich bank. This was certainly not a novel request, and, after comparing signatures, the New York bank sent a draft to the Zurich bank as requested.

Four days later another New York bank received a letter from Paris, asking that twenty thousand dollars be transferred to a Paris bank. This depositor lived in Buenos Aires, Argentina. The bank complied.

Then, on February 3, a Long Island bank had a letter post-marked Brussels, Belgium, signed by a depositor whose home was in Sao Paulo, Brazil, requesting that ten thousand dollars be transferred by telegram to a Brussels bank. This bank was more fortunate. The depositor normally had less than two thousand dollars in his account. However, a check for fourteen thousand dollars had recently been deposited. But the bank elected to wait until the check cleared, which took ten days. When the check cleared, the Long Island bank asked a New York bank to handle the transfer, because it did not have a foreign-exchange depart-ment. By this time some of the fraudulent transactions had come to light, and the New York bank advised Long Island to check with its

Brazilian depositor before sending any money to Europe. When the Brazilian was reached in Sao Paulo—not in Brussels, as presumed—he said he certainly had made no request for any transfer of funds to Europe.

Faced with a king-size problem, the banks asked postal inspectors whether the mails could contribute to such a far-flung fraud. It seemed all too clear to the postal inspectors that someone working in the Sao Paulo and Buenos Aires post offices was stealing bank statements and other correspondence between wealthy depositors in Brazil and Argentina and banks in New York and vicinity. The mail would then be examined by members of the gang. Those with large accounts in banks were selected and their mail photostated. The original letters would be carefully resealed and returned to the mail as quickly as possible to avoid any suspicion.

With this information, forged letters of demand were sent to the New York banks as quickly as possible. Investigators soon learned that demands had been made on at least ten banks within a period of little more than a week.

The photostats of the stolen mail would show the gang how much each depositor had in his account, copies of his signature, and other information. Using this material, confederates in Europe were able to get phony identification of various kinds, including passports with their own photographs in the names of the depositors. Then gang members needed only to open a bank account and to practice writing the depositor's signature until it could be done so well that even an expert would have difficulty detecting the forgery. As quickly as funds were transferred, one member of the gang in Europe would withdraw the money and move along.

The inspectors' part in solving the case was all done at a desk where, with knowledge of how the mail was worked and moved, they charted out each mail theft and quickly provided Interpol, the banks, and foreign investigators in several different countries with the vital information that enabled them to arrest the widely separated conspirators.

Then there are those who find a certain fascination in chain letters. Chain letters often appear to be an easy way to parlay some small change into thousands of dollars. The gimmick requires no monetary risk to speak of, just a little effort writing letters and a few postage stamps. You simply send a dime to the person whose name appears at the top of a list, put your name at the bottom, and send off five or six letters. Then you wait for your name to reach the top and gather your reward in hundreds of letters coming to you, each with a dime.

Chain letters of one kind or another have been around for years, but they usually wear themselves out before they go very far. The summer of 1933 was different. It was the year of the big chain-letter mania. The Great Depression of 1929–1932 was at last starting to release its grip; people were losing their fears and regaining some confidence. The sudden chain-letter activity was either a barometer of better times to come or a last-gasp effort to turn total poverty into riches.

Reports of people receiving huge volumes of mail containing dimes spread like wildfire. Reports of bushel baskets of mail being delivered to a few lucky individuals were repeated over and over. People forgot the depression, and almost everyone tried to get in on the sudden bonanza.

The post offices, where the craze was particularly hot, were glutted with mail where there had been little for years. Extra letter carriers had to be hired to deliver the deluge of chain letters, and additional clerks were needed to sort the mail. Some of those hired to help out were people who had been out of work for two or three years. It was a carnival spirit, and a contagious one.

At first the chain letters asked for only a dime; but soon this seemed too small, and so some chains started asking for quarters, half-dollars, one-dollar bills, fives, tens, and even twenties. The money, hidden for so long, was flushed back into circulation. The spirits, if not the finances, of many were boosted overnight.

As so often happens when people begin to feel they have come across a good thing, someone has to spoil all the fun. This time it was the postal inspectors, who warned that chain letters were a form of lottery, and so mailing them was illegal. These announcements failed to frighten most, but they did have the sobering effect of making some people pause to think how impossible the whole chain-letter scheme really was. It just couldn't work out so that everyone would really get thousands of dollars for an investment of ten cents.

Many can remember how the chains worked. You would receive a letter in the mail containing a list of five or six names with their addresses. You were to remove the name from the top of the list and send ten cents to that person. Then you wrote five letters to others, moving each name up on the list and adding your name to the bottom of the list.

"When your name reaches the top of the list, you will receive over fifteen hundred dollars in dimes. Do not break the chain. It is bad luck. One lady in Iowa broke the chain and suffered a bad accident a day later." This and similar wording carried both a promise and a warning.

Soon many began to try to speed up or beat the course of the chain. They might slip their names in ahead of others, hoping to make less but to get what they could sooner. Others would send out far more copies than asked for, hoping to double or to triple their returns.

Soon people were in on so many chains and were mailing so many chain letters that they found it hard to squeeze in the time to write the chain letters. Local printers were quick to start printing chain-letter forms, where the buyer needed only to write in the names of those on the list and then to mail the form. Almost any denomination-form chain letter could be purchased. Some printers made these forms up in volume and hired boys to sell them on the street corners in the larger cities. Everybody seemed to be working again, for a while.

As the chain fad wore on, it became evident that not everyone in on the chains was doing what should be done. Soon chain letter shops were opened in some of the vacant buildings in the cities. Here your original investment was supposed to be protected, and the U. S. Mail was not used. You simply went into a shop and put your money down. It was given to the person whose name was at the top of the particular chain you bought into. Then you waited until enough people came into the "club" to work your name to the top of the list.

One such chain-letter shop was opened at 1809 Curtis Street in Denver, Colorado. It was called the "Prosperity Club." The one dollar you invested was supposed to pay eighty-one dollars after 120 people followed you, each with their dollar. In this "three" combination, your original investment of one dollar went to a name on top of the list. After three more people invested in your chain, your name advanced one step up the chain. It took nine more to move you up another step, and the next twenty-seven moved your name to the magic spot. You were then the one whose name was on the top of the list. Now, all it took was eighty-one people to invest a dollar, and then you would receive your eighty-one dollars, less a commission for handling. When this was completed, your name went off the list.

This made sense to a lot of people, but the police bunco squads didn't buy it. They were no more understanding than the postal inspectors had been about mailing chain letters.

Some skeptics could see through the whole thing and sent out chain letters asking friends to send their wives to the person whose name was at the top of a list. These letters promised that if the chain was not broken, you would soon have at least nine hundred wives. This type of chain letter explained the scheme more completely than any postal inspector or bunco squad ever could. After all, who besides Solomon could suffer that many wives?

Attempts are often made to avoid using the mails because of the fraud and lottery statutes. The following chain letter waved the flag by using U.S. Savings Bonds, and it promised that the operation was legal. Such schemes are not legal if the mail is used at any point in the operation. In this case, bonds were mailed in furtherance of the scheme, although the chain letter itself was not mailed. Consequently, the operation was subject to prosecution under the federal law.

(1.) You give $37.50 by hand to the person giving you this list of names. He gives you a $25.00 savings bond in the name of the person whose name is first on the list you have purchased.

(2.) Don't use the mail to send your list. It is illegal to do so.

(3.) Make two identical copies of this letter, eliminating the top name and adding your name and address to the bottom. Thus, the name which originally was No. 1, is removed. Thus, No. 2 is No. 1, and your name is No. 10.

(4.) The name on the bond is the same as the name at the top of the list you have just purchased. Mail the bond at once to the person whose name is on the bond. It is legal to do so.

(5.) Purchase from the bank two (2) $25.00 savings bonds made out to the person whose name comes first on the list you have just made out. You sell each list with bond attached for $37.50. You have your money back.

(6.) When your name reaches the top of the list, you should receive thirty-eight thousand dollars in savings bonds, worth fifty thousand dollars at maturity. This campaign is surefire, because each person will hasten to get his money back, moving your name on up the list. Responsible legal talent has advised that this procedure of selling government bonds is legal. This also benefits your country.

This was a chain letter that exhibited some thought and planning. The person who set it up tried to cover all angles as best he could. If he played it straight and started with a list of close friends or associates, he could have made a bundle. After all, he was in on the ground floor, and those who followed him would be the losers. One thing that makes chain letters interesting is the speculation about just how much the originator of a good chain letter actually got away with.

In another case, an international chain-letter fraud got off to a very bleak and jarring start when one of the letters was received by Lee W. Robertson, a postal inspector in New Orleans.

It was Valentines Day, February 14, 1966, and Robertson opened his post office box on his way up to his office when he went to work that morning. The Valentine that Robertson received didn't have a heart, and there was no poetry. It was a chain letter mailed from Santiago, Chile, addressed to "Box holder," New Orleans.

It was a typical chain, with six names requesting that ten dollars be sent to the name at the top of the list. The receiver was asked to write five identical letters to friends, eliminating the name at the top of the list and adding his own at the bottom. He was assured of soon getting $31,250. All this for ten dollars and a little letter writing.

Having an inquiring mind—one of the prime requisites for anyone in his line of work—Robertson immediately began poking around in the other post office boxes. Here he found two thousand identical letters, all postmarked Santiago, Chile, waiting in boxes ready for New Orleans's box holders. The letters were declared unmailable and seized, thereby saving the people of New Orleans a few dollars.

It also occurred to Inspector Robertson that New Orleans might not be the only city receiving these letters. The chief inspector was contacted, and he notified other post offices throughout the country. By the next day twenty-five thousand identical chain letters had been intercepted in twenty cities.

It was found that the six names listed on the chain letters meant little, except the first two. The third name was that of a dead man. The first name was Spanish, with an address of a savings-and-loan association's post office box in San Gabriel, California. The second name carried the address of a savings-and-loan association in Nassau, Bahamas, The savings-and-loan association in San Gabriel had received a request by mail from Chile to open an account and deposit all funds received by mail into that account.

The operator had set himself up for a half million in a fast chain-letter operation and obviously planned to be gone before the third name on the chain-letter list ever reached the top. He may even have had visions of just staying in the Bahamas.

Again, in 1970, Inspector Kenneth Ishmael in Oklahoma was investigating a one-dollar chain letter that had started in Knoxville, Tennessee, and had spread quickly through Florida and Texas before it came to the inspector's attention in Oklahoma City. The chain promised eight thousand dollars for one dollar, an enticing offer. However, it was found that one of the chain letters had six names, all of which were actually the same person using different pen names and different addresses and drops. This man wasn't taking any chances with the chain-letter cheats—he wanted all the action. His greed caused Inspector Ishmael to present the matter to Assistant U.S. Attorney John E. Green for prosecution under the federal mail-fraud statutes.

How can a chain-letter operation ever be stopped when it has new names supposedly coming into it every time one is mailed? No one seems to know why they start or why they stop. Chain letters have a way of just fading into dark recesses, where they remain until their own particular springtime tells them it is time again to come forth, to grow, to bloom, to bestow their wealth upon the few, to accept the pennies of the hopeful, then slowly to wilt and to go to seed to await the next cycle of man's gulosity.

Selling distributorships is another one of the many ways to pick someone's pocket and frequently supports the old saying "There is a sucker born every minute!"

Remember those old advertisements that offered gadgets or motors guaranteed to save vast amounts of gasoline? Years ago the Jet Engine Company offered a gas turbine capable of driving a car 250 miles on a single gallon of crude oil. Their advertisement in a scientific publication said so! "Imagine 250 miles per gallon your car now. Literature 25¢, Jet Engine Co., St. Augustine, Florida."

Now that we need it, whatever happened to this wonderful machine? Did the "big boys" buy up the patent and bury it? Could it just be possible the answer lies buried in the land of Ponce de Leon's fountain of youth? No way.

Like Ponce de Leon, the postal inspectors of the fraud unit went to St. Augustine in 1948 after this enticing advertisement appeared. They found some fascinating things in St. Augustine, but no jet engine.

The letterhead of the Jet Engine Company listed names of several officers and research engineers associated with the company, but the owner and inventor Jess C. Thomas turned out to be a part-time musician, and his research engineers consisted of a clerk who was employed by the National Park Service and a bookkeeper who worked in a local ice plant. This crew constituted the technical staff.

Still searching for at least a fountain of truth, the inspectors found that the engine had never been perfected. Thomas claimed to have conducted experiments on the engine but had dismantled it because of imperfections. He showed them a cardboard box containing pieces of pipe and metal, which he claimed had been the actual working model. He had sets of plans showing details of the jet engine.

Thomas had sold exclusive distributorships to about twenty victims who had responded to his advertisements. The U.S. Mail had been used, and the inspectors suspected the entire operation was a violation of the mail-fraud statutes. Throughout the many years of its existence, the Postal Inspection Service had always been very cognizant of consumer protection whenever the mails were used in a scheme. On the face of it, they didn't think Thomas's jet engine measured up to his claims at all.

Copies of the plans were sent to the National Bureau of Standards and to Hoyt C. Hottel of the Massachusetts Institute of Technology. Hottel was recognized at the time as an outstanding authority on jet propulsion engines. After looking over the plans and reading Thomas's literature, they reported that he had no basis for making claims he had advertised. In fact, they said that any jet engine constructed from those plans would be worthless, much less a gas saver.

Thomas was indicted and pled not guilty to charges of mail fraud. A trial was held, but after the first witness had testified against him, he changed his plea to guilty. The court asked if he had anything to say before being sentenced. Not one to give up easily, Thomas told the judge that he could bring his jet engine into the courtroom, when he had it together, and prove that it would operate. The judge, apparently not disposed to wait until Thomas got it all together, sentenced him to serve a year and a day.

Now, with environment and energy foremost in the thoughts of most of us, wouldn't it be interesting to locate Mr. Thomas and learn whether he had finally put his jet engine together and had it working? He had claimed many revolutionary things. He had stated his engine would operate on crude oil; that it ran from 100 to 250 miles on only one gallon of oil; that it gave smoothness of operation with no vibration; that it could be installed to fit any automobile or truck using about one hundred horsepower; that no hot gases came out the exhaust pipe; that the engine was quiet, smooth, cool, and efficient.

Thomas also mentioned that three automobile manufacturers were interested in the jet engine as standard equipment of the future. That was about twenty-five years ago, and its use is still in the future as standard equipment so far as anyone knows. Looking at the matter objectively, how much do we really need a fountain of youth or an inventor with a dismantled motor in a cardboard box? However, it would certainly solve some chronic and acute problems.

12

The Beauty Queen and Other Quacks

You can expect to live longer and more comfortably than the average woman in any era since time began, thanks to the miracle of modern science. But you can also expect to outlive your beauty.

Will you become one of those tragic women with the lines of age in their faces, the drooping cheeks, the puffy eyes, the wrinkled necks? Are you unhappy with your present physical appearance? Do you dread the bitter years, the downhill road?

Believe me, there is another road, the road marked 'Hope.' And this is my personal message to you: Your face can regain the loveliness of youth through facial rejuvenation without surgery. The decades ahead can be dynamic and productive. Yours can be a more beautiful tomorrow.

THUS READ THE enchanting international advertisements of Cora Galenti, one of the most ruthless, unscrupulous, and cruel fraud artists who ever preyed upon the fraility of human vanity.

Madame Galenti offered solace through the restoration of youth to those who, like Ponce de Leon, were searching for the elusive fountain of youth. She called the clinic she operated in her palatial home near Las Vegas, Nevada, the Fountain of Youth Ranch.

Cora Galenti was an attractive blonde in her sixties. She enticed those who had managed to survive the varied assaults of time and who, upon looking into the mirror, wistfully yearned to regain the youthful fresh look they once enjoyed. Even at three thousand dollars a treatment, many were a ripe mark for the madame's "magic formula." In fact, over the years it is estimated she treated over three thousand patients.

On September 22, 1961, her ranch-type clinic was raided, and she was arrested for practicing medicine without a license. A search of her home resulted in the seizure of her deeply guarded secret formula for youth. It was a solution of carbolic acid.

The nonsurgical therapy performed by Galenti, who had no medical training, consisted of several applications of a 48 percent solution of phenol (carbolic acid) to the face and neck of the victims.

Phenol is an acid extremely painful to the skin. In three weeks of almost constant applications, the acid simply burned off the outer layer of skin, wrinkles and all. The toxic acid burns and blisters any area it touches. With the face and neck packed with her formula and swathed in bandages, heavy sedation was necessary during treatment.

The legendary Greek enchantress Circe changed men into swine. Enchantress Galenti changed the complexions of her patients into splotchy patches of color like a pinto pony, with ridges of puckered flesh like a toad. Needless to say, her practice didn't thrive on referral recommendations.

Many people will endure enormous pain and physical torture for the sake of youthful beauty. With the madame, the pain and torture was ample, but the results were a disaster. One thirty-five-year-old professional dancer who took the treatment was so terribly disfigured she committed suicide.

Many victims were reluctant to complain publicly and to admit that their vanity had led them to take such a disasterous step. Galenti, relying on this reluctance, was able to operate from about 1950 until 1960 before postal inspectors had complaints. She certainly had used the mails in her freewheeling advertising.

In 1960, Los Angeles postal inspectors found sufficient evidence to request a fraud order denying her the use of the mails in the promotion of her business. She easily avoided this by signing a stipulation agreeing to discontinue the solicitation by mail of her clinical beauty treatments. She never honored this promise. She was also arrested twice in Los Angeles for practicing medicine without a license. She paid her fine and went back to her lucrative practice.

It wasn't until some of her patients in California brought disfigurement suits that she moved her operations to Nevada.

When she was arrested at her ranch near Las Vegas, the only charges the local officials could bring against her were misdemeanor charges; but they did have some hard evidence, her secret formula, phenol. They turned to the postal inspectors for help under the mail-fraud statutes.

By this time, damage suits totalling nearly two million dollars had been brought against the madame. Through these suits witnesses were interviewed, and ten victims ultimately testified at her trial for violation of the mail-fraud statutes.

Galenti was sentenced in Las Vegas on October 28, 1962, to five years' imprisonment and was released on seventy-five hundred dollars bail, pending appeal. She promptly moved to San Diego and went right back into practice. When the court of appeals upheld her conviction, Galenti jumped bail and flew to Mexico City.

Although married, the madame soon found a suitable Mexican national and married him, which gave her sanctuary. Fraud violations are not extraditable in Mexico, so she was safe from postal inspectors, immigration authorities, and justice.

It wasn't long before the madame was back in business in Tijuana, just south of the California border, where those in the United States who wanted treatments could readily obtain them. She was still doing business south of the border as late as 1966, but reports indicated that her business was slow.

If there was any reason for her ruthlessness, it was because she was a compulsive high-stake gambler, but she was not nearly the gambler each of her patients was.

Many others have found quackery a lucrative field. Barking his miracle cure for every ailment, the medicine man is gone from the scene, but he once toured our country in a wagon making one-night stands in towns and villages. His nostrums, frequently laced with alcohol and sometimes with opium, were supposedly concocted from bark, roots, or herbs under secret formulas learned from the Indians or handed down through the centuries.

In rare cases a few of the ingredients used did have some beneficial medicinal properties, and a few are marketed today in a refined form, but they are not ballyhooed from a wagon. Television reaches far more people. Most of the medicine man's tonics and pills were little more than placebos. The last medicine show I saw was in Amarillo, Texas, on a warm night in the summer of 1930. While my attention was on the show, someone stole the spare tire from the back of my 1927 Ford coupe with a rumble seat.

A continuing dream of good health creates lucrative markets for such things as blackstrap molasses, wheat germ, yogurt, vitamins, and minerals. Many fraudulent cures are sold or promoted through the mail.

Postal inspectors have been watching medical-fraud artists for years. Some are heartless swindlers, motivated by dishonesty and greed, who prey upon agonized victims who are in a desperate search for freedom from pain, disease, and death.

The "You are what you eat" pitch was used by an unscrupulous chemist to increase the sales of a vitamin manufacturer. He claimed that good health is totally dependent upon a hormone balance, which could be measured by urine analysis. A laboratory was set up, and between 1950 and 1965 ailing persons were frightened into spending eight million dollars for unneeded vitamins and three million dollars for fake urine analysis.

After complaints began to come in, postal inspectors mailed eight samples of colored distilled water to the laboratory as a test. All eight reports came back indicating sizable hormone deficiencies. The fake analysis contributed to the arrest of the chemist, the vitamin manufacturer, and the laboratory operator. All entered a plea of guilty of mail fraud.

Machines are often a favorite of the quack. One was an electrical device called the Magnetron, a cabinet contraption that was sold for $197.50 by a seventy-eight-year-old osteopath. Plugged into an ordinary house current, the panel lit up brightly while the patient grasped one electrode and placed his or her foot on an attachment pad. It was advertised to cure varicose veins, prostate difficulty, arthritis, ulcers, diabetes, failing heart, and bleeding piles—a real broadside remedy for whatever ails you. Actually, the machine supplied somewhat less heat than one would experience sleeping under an electric blanket. Over three hundred Magnetrons were sold to ailing people, some in pitiful condition, before the doctor was brought to trial. During the trial, he was ordered to stop selling the machines.

Strangely, when about fifty buyers of the Magnetrons were interviewed, the typical response was "wouldn't be without it" or "it is less expensive than visiting a doctor where nothing is administered but those long needles."

Then there was the fake chiropractor who devised a colonic irrigation machine he called the Dexoxacolon. He claimed that "all diseases have their root in the colon, and that water mixed with oxygen would effect a cure for almost every ailment." He sold his machines for twenty-five hundred dollars each to chiropractors.

He would visit a town and make a deal with a chiropractor, whereby he would give "free" examinations, which were announced by mail. After a physical examination and X ray that cost the victim ten dollars, he would point out serious disorders, including malignancies. He would guarantee a cure if the patient would take weekly treatments on the Dexoxacolon for a fee of $350. After a week of signing up victims, the "doctor" would depart with a percentage of the advances and the sale price of the Dexoxacolon.

Using the mails to circularize prospective patients brought the postal inspectors into the operation. They found that in one case he had told a woman that her X ray showed a malignant kidney, whereas the X ray did not show the kidney area at all. This is the kind of evidence a jury can get a handle on. After bilking and hastening the death of many trusting persons, he was brought to trial and given a ten-year sentence in a federal penitentiary for mail fraud.

In another case there was an interesting fellow who sold a nostrum that was positively guaranteed to grow hair. Less harmful, this operation had its appeal to male vanity. Possibly the reason he was never brought to trial was that the inspector sent to investigate was bald. We were always suspicious that the inspector was eternally hopeful that the bottled juice might just possibly encourage a little hair on his own bald pate. The operator has long since gone out of business, giving final evidence that his hair restorer just wasn't the proper fertilizer for hair growth.

13

The Postal Posse

WHEN TWO OR MORE postal inspectors get together, there are two cases they like to talk about.

One such case is called the Great Plymouth Mail Robbery and the other is the murder and mail holdup at Guthrie, Kentucky.

One case occurred almost a quarter of a century after the other, but both presented unusual and interesting twists that kept the inspectors busy for months as they met one frustration after the other on the road toward catching the bandits.

A most extensive manhunt began after three men jumped out of a car on January 5, 1938, in Guthrie, Kentucky, and fired a burst from a machine gun, which killed mail messenger Arthur Mimms, who was carrying registered mail containing twenty-five thousand dollars in currency from the post office to the railroad depot to dispatch on a train.

Mimms was accompanied by Chief of Police C. M. Sherrod and a post office clerk. Chief Sherrod was wounded in the leg. The badly frightened clerk was roughly shoved into the bandits' car along with the currency shipment, and the holdup men drove out of town at high speed. A few miles out of town the clerk was thrown out of the car. He was not badly hurt.

The chief called the county sheriff and notified the postal inspectors from the hospital where he was taken. Chief Inspector K. P. Aldrich took charge of a case that was to become a nationwide manhunt.

Among the first postal inspectors to reach Guthrie were Hartley B. Dean, F. D. McMahon, and Inspector in Charge W. R. Briggs of the Cincinnati Division. I can remember Inspector Dean later telling of the months he and McMahon spent on the case and the miles he traveled chasing the dangerous holdup men. Before it was over, many inspectors were to spend many weeks away from home, following leads that usually never worked out in the case.

The post office clerk who had been shoved into the getaway car was the first witness to be interviewed. He was able to give a good description of the bandits. The sheriff had set up roadblocks and had notified all surrounding law enforcement people, but the bandits slipped through the dragnet.

Then came the first break. Two weeks before the holdup, the village blacksmith, George W. Winn, was working in his shop, which was located across from the railroad depot. He happened to notice a car parked nearby with four men in it. Strangers were not too common in Guthrie, and Smithy Winn supposed the men were having car trouble.

After a while, his curiosity got the better of him and he went out and asked the men if he could be of any help. This seemed to startle the men, and one of them told him to mind his own business and to beat it.

People around Guthrie didn't usually react that way when approached in a friendly manner. Winn went back to his smithy. After thinking about it, he looked out the window and took down the license number of the car, noting that it was a Ford. This happened, he told the inspectors, about two weeks before the holdup.

The law enforcement people suspected that the men in the car parked near the depot about train time could be the holdup trio casing the job. Inspector in Charge Archie A. Imus, in Chicago, was asked to get the make on the Illinois license number. He came back with the information that the license was issued to a George Taylor for a Buick car.

The blacksmith had said the car they were driving was a Ford, not a Buick. At first no one seemed to have any idea who or where

194

George Taylor might be. Numerous law enforcement people and the inspectors began to check hotel registrations throughout five states. This tedious task brought results, and the name George Taylor began to turn up on several hotel registers, usually accompanied with a W. Taylor.

Even in those days, law enforcement agents had a file on known burglars and heavies. It was little trouble to find that George and W. Taylor were actually the infamous Bruce brothers—Floyd, age thirty-seven; and Ray, age twenty-nine. Floyd, considered to be the leader of the two, had aliases E. F. Bruce, George Miller, George Taylor, George Bronson, B. F. Edwards, and George King.

Ray Bruce went under the names W. Taylor, Ray Foster, W. Foster, Jimmy King, Ray Bronson, Roy Harrison, Edgar Shaw, J. A. Williams, and Jimmy Culpepper.

The Bruce brothers were wanted for several jobs, including the kidnapping of a federal officer and a factory-payroll holdup. Floyd Bruce was an escapee from a Georgia chain gang. The two were known hijackers and bootleggers, suspected of working with the notorious Chicago Beer Baron, Bugsy Moran.

Their handwriting from hotel registers compared with known writing at prisons was found to be identical. Prison pictures were shown to Chief Sherrod and the post office clerk in Guthrie, who positively identified the pair. This was enough to obtain an indictment, and the inspectors started printing wanted circulars that would be shown in every post office, hotel, filling station, and other logical places in the area.

Finally, the wanted circulars began to pay off. Out of hundreds of false leads, one report was received indicating that Floyd Bruce was operating a filling station far away in San Antonio, Texas. Rushing a force composed of postal inspectors, local police, and Texas Rangers, the pursuers found that they were holding an empty bag. Floyd had sold the filling station two weeks before and was off again. He had been there five months.

Soon another tip indicated that Ray Bruce was running a chicken farm in Florida. Another hurried dragnet and another empty net. He had gone, but he had run the chicken farm for several months.

With the knowledge that both Bruce brothers were on the move again, it was expected that they might be planning to team up. The inspectors were hot on their trail but always just a little behind them, it seemed.

In comparing notes with others, Inspectors E. J. Holmes and J. A. Thompson learned that Floyd Bruce had purchased a new car in San Antonio, which he used to drive to Springfield, Missouri.

In Springfield, Missouri, he abandoned the car he had bought in San Antonio, bought a new one, and drove it to Springfield, Illinois. When he reached Springfield, Illinois, he again abandoned the new car he had recently bought, then bought still another new car. It was later learned that he always kept the license plates so that he could change plates frequently.

This was about the most expensive way to travel that had yet been tried in those days of hot cars, hot women, and hot rods. It was also an effective way to throw off your pursuers if you could stand the price.

Floyd was on his third new car when his luck ran out. He and his woman companion were staying at a tourist home in Normal, Illinois. Here the landlady recognized Floyd Bruce from a wanted circular she had received, but she was afraid to call the police while he was at her place for fear of a shoot-out.

The next morning, when Bruce and his lady started to leave, he couldn't get his car started. He asked a salesman, who was also staying at the tourist home, for a push. Still the car wouldn't start, and so the salesman pushed the car as far as a filling station. The salesman then went back to the tourist home and told the landlady he was sure the man was Floyd Bruce and to call the police. When he got her call, Chief C. Y. Lee called Bloomington for reinforcements and drove near the filling station to a spot where he could watch Floyd without arousing his suspicion.

Postal Inspectors Holmes and L. C. Kirkpatrick were in Bloomington running down tips. They joined Inspectors F. C. Courtney and E. E. Harding and hurried to Normal. A posse was formed at the Normal police station made up of postal inspectors and police officers under the leadership of Inspector Holmes.

Floyd was standing near the car at the time this force arrived, watching the serviceman who was working on the motor. When Floyd saw the posse approaching, he reached into his pocket, but he changed his mind and held up his hands. He was heavily armed with a .45 caliber automatic and a .38 caliber revolver on his person. In the car was a .357 caliber rifle and a submachine gun. He could see there were just too many guns pointing at him. His new car bore Tennessee license plates. His woman companion was released, and Floyd was charged in federal court in Louisville, Kentucky, for armed robbery of the mail.

Ray Bruce was still at large, and so the hunt went on. Ray had found a hideout of sorts near Ellaville, Georgia, where he was staying with the Jordan family, who had a farm nearby. Ray might have been safe out there, but one day he took a machine gun out of his car and started to take it apart and clean it on the kitchen table. This aroused the suspicions of Jordan, who wrote a note to the sheriff, telling him how Ray had asked for a place to rest but was just now cleaning a machine gun in the Jordan kitchen. He sent the message to town by his eleven-year-old son.

When the sheriff read the note, he showed the boy some wanted circulars, including the one the inspectors had out for the Bruce brothers. The boy identified Ray's picture as the man living with the Jordan family.

The sheriff wrote a note to the boy's father, telling him to quietly move the family into one of the barns and that upon a signal he should tell Ray Bruce the place was surrounded and to leave the house with his hands up.

The sheriff quickly formed a posse of state and local lawmen, including Inspectors R. D. Greer, E. E. Harding, and F. D. McMahon, who were all in the community because they had heard that Ray was in the vicinity. When they reached the farm, the sheriff signaled the farmer by waving a handkerchief on a stick from behind a nearby stump. Out of the house came Jordan, who stopped about ten feet from the door and shouted for Bruce to give up, that the place was surrounded. The moment of truth had come for Ray Bruce. Was he to make a stand? He had exactly the same kinds of weapons as his brother, but he decided against making a stand and came out with his hands up.

What about the third man in the holdup? A month after the holdup, an informant told the inspectors that the man was Ernest Morris, who had just stored his car in a garage at Madisonville, Kentucky. Morris was known as a gunman from prohibition days and was considered dangerous.

The only thing to do was to maintain a twenty-four-hour, day-by-day watch over the garage in hope that he would return for his car.

The alley leading to the garage was wired, and floodlights were installed on nearby telephone poles so that the entire area could be brightly lit by flipping a switch inside the garage door. Then inspectors took shifts, standing by the light switch and watching the alley, waiting day after day for over three weeks.

Their efforts were rewarded the night of April 10, when someone stealthily entered the alley about eleven in the evening. The officers' guns were drawn and they waited until the man neared the garage door, then Inspector McMahon, who was on the shift, threw the switch. "We are government officers. Throw up your hands, Morris," he said. The man turned in the direction of the voice and pulled out two guns. He didn't get a chance to shoot. The lawmen shot first, and Morris fell dead. His picture was later shown to Chief of Police Sherrod of Guthrie and the post office clerk, both of whom identified him as the third man in the Guthrie holdup.

A jury in Bowling Green, Kentucky, found Floyd and Ray Bruce guilty after being out only thirty minutes. Judge MacSwinford sentenced each one to serve fifty-seven years. They were tried in May 1939, sixteen months after the holdup, which shows that justice can move swiftly on occasion.

"Stand and deliver!" was the command given when the masked bandits held up the old Overland or Wells Fargo stages in the 1860s. The stage stopped, the strongbox was kicked off, the travelers were relieved of their valuables, and the boys in the black hats rode off into the hills.

A posse was formed, and a chase frequently ended in catching the bandits. Not too far away was a tall tree where the bandits were strung up, or so it has often been portrayed in Western folklore.

A hundred years later the mail stage and mail train robberies were upstaged by what has been called the Great Plymouth Mail Robbery, which netted the modern-day bandits over one and a half million in small, unmarked bills. The bandits were not all men—at least one woman was involved in the holdup. A great deal of evidence was eventually gathered, but it took a long time and a great deal of hard work before those suspected were brought before justice.

The Great Plymouth Mail Robbery took place on Tuesday evening August 14, 1962, in the Cape Cod area of Massachusetts. The persons who cased this job couldn't have had too much trouble figuring out how and when to hold up the mail truck. Many tourists visit Cape Cod during the summer months and spend heavily, particularly over a weekend. It followed that there must be a surplus of money in the area by Monday. It also followed that the merchants would take the profits to their banks on Monday and that the banks would need to ship a large sum out to the Federal Reserve Bank in Boston on Tuesday. This seemed obvious, and, as it turned out, it was the procedure followed. Later investigation determined that several gangs had been studying the possibilities for a long time.

Having settled on what the banks did, the next problem was how to take the mail truck carrying the excess currency. If the plan they finally worked out proceeded smoothly, no one would be shot, killed, or hurt.

Mail being transported on the Hyannis via Buzzards Bay to Boston route was carried in regular post office trucks instead of by private trucks normally used by mail contractors on routes like this. This would make the truck hauling the currency very easy to recognize as it came along the highway.

Also, it is the usual practice in cases where valuable mail is being hauled on a route to ask the state police to convoy these shipments. In this case the holdup men found out by observation, or were told

199

by an accomplice, that the convoy protection given these shipments was at best limited to occasional random spot checks along the route.

The holdup was planned carefully and was well executed. The plan of action was both simple and effective. Official detour and roadblock signs were stolen and fabricated, then set up on the evening of the holdup immediately after the mail truck passed a fork in the main highway. This diverted all traffic to a side road so that the holdup would proceed smoothly without the danger of some unsuspecting driver coming upon the scene during the actual crime.

The driver of the mail truck would later remember that the only vehicle that passed them in this stretch of road was a speeding Oldsmobile, which passed just before they were stopped. This car probably carried the men who set up the roadblock behind the mail truck.

Soon after the Oldsmobile passed, the driver saw two Oldsmobiles alongside the highway. As he approached, one of the cars pulled across the highway in front of the mail truck. A man masquerading as a policeman in full uniform with white gloves held up his hand and stopped the truck.

Neither the driver of the mail truck, Patrick Schena, nor guard William F. Barrett suspected foul play until two men dressed as policemen approached both sides of the mail truck with shotguns. They were ordered to open the door and to lie facedown on the floor in the rear of the truck. They offered no resistance. They were relieved of the .38 caliber revolvers they had been issued and were bound with tape.

Schena and Barrett reported that after they were bound, the truck was driven over what seemed to be a dirt road for about fifteen minutes. When it stopped, several of the mailbags were passed out to a silent conspirator, after which it proceeded a little farther along and made another stop, where the balance of the mail sacks was passed out. The two holdup men were the only ones who did any talking, and they called each other by the names of Buster and Tony.

When the mail was all disposed of, the truck was driven still farther along. Then the holdup men stopped and got out, warning Schena and Barrett not to get up.

As soon as the two could break free of their bonds, they climbed out of the truck and found themselves on Route 128 in the outskirts of Boston. They were soon able to flag down a young foreign student on a motorcycle, who turned in the alarm.

It was only a short time before the area was full of state and local police, FBI agents, and postal inspectors. The immediate dragnet was fruitless. Evidence was being gathered by several different agencies without any central direction, each believing it was doing what it should and each wanting to solve the case. The postal inspector in charge at Boston actually had primary jurisdiction in any investigation of this nature. He was asked by the chief inspector to call a meeting of all law enforcement agencies involved, to request their cooperation, and to inform them that the postal inspectors had primary jurisdiction. When this was done it was possible to coordinate the hard work of the investigation.

Of course it was a big case and it was news. The press was trying to get the facts about the heist, and they heard a variety of stories from the various law enforcement agencies. Even after the inspectors were given jurisdiction, the press found the Boston office was not very inclined to give them many particulars. This probably provoked them into venting their frustrations on the Post Office Department for its careless handling of valuable registered shipments of currency and on the Inspection Service for its slow progress in solving the case.

Gone was one and a half million dollars in unidentifiable small bills. Gone were the two men dressed in police uniforms. Gone was a woman who was believed to have driven one of the Oldsmobiles that had had several sacks of the mail transferred to it along the dirt road.

The long hard task of putting the evidence together, identifying those responsible for the holdup, and presenting the case for prosecution fell to the postal inspectors. Off and on for the ensuing two years, some eighty postal inspectors were assigned to the case in the Boston area alone.

Schena and Barrett were able to give a fair description of the two who held them up, and from this an artist drew a sketch of two holdup men who called each other by the names Buster and Tony. From this sketch a wanted circular was issued.

The traffic cones used at the barricade, a yellow sign reading WORK AREA AHEAD, two MEN IN ROAD signs—one of which was covered with a cardboard DETOUR sign—and a metal DANGER sign with a broken reflector were gathered and retained for evidence. Two Oldsmobiles used in the holdup were abandoned, and it was found that both had been stolen. Another Oldsmobile was found partially burned and abandoned in Boston. It was believed to be the car used to receive some of the mail sacks containing currency that were passed out of the mail truck on the dirt road.

The investigation then settled down to the hard work of identifying those responsible. The chief inspector sent his best criminal investigators to Boston and put all the manpower he could spare into the case. The investigation covered a wide span of possibilities. Countless postal employees, contract mail drivers, Massachusetts State and other police officers, and many who might have even a remote knowledge of the holdup had to be talked to.

As in all big cases that generate publicity, this case caused many people to come forth with what they thought, or imagined, to be leads. Every one of these had to be checked out. Inspectors working on this case estimated that the names of approximately two thousand persons were turned in from various sources as suspected accomplices in the holdup.

One of the first important steps was to interview all known major felons and holdup men in the area on the theory that one of them might drop a piece of information that would serve as a clue to the identity of the holdup gang. This important phase of the work went to five teams of inspectors, two on each team. One team interviewed a known holdup man called Billy the Greek, who was in prison for bank robbery.

Billy the Greek was a long-time crime partner of John J. Kelley, who had once been found guilty of possession of stolen money from an armed robbery of a Belmont, Massachusetts, bank. It was also learned that these two had developed Thomas R. Richards as an accomplice.

Richards had no criminal record and was steadily employed. In other words, he was clean. Allegedly he was used to hold caches of weapons and loot, frequently going along on jobs as a driver.

When Billy the Greek was interviewed, he said that he was not pleased with the way he had been treated by John J. Kelley. Kelley had not visited him in prison, and the gang was not financially supporting his family while he served time. Billy told inspectors that the bank heist for which he was serving time involved both Kelley and Richards, whom he had covered up for. He complained that he had never received any of the bank loot. These things motivated Billy to tell what he knew about the Great Plymouth Mail Robbery and to disclose the identity of those involved.

Under the circumstances, the inspectors asked Billy to take a lie-detector examination covering those he named. The test indicated Billy truly believed Kelley and Richards were involved in the Plymouth holdup. Richards was suspected of hiding the bulk of the loot in his home. With this vital intelligence, the case was essentially broken, but the hard work had just begun.

It would seem simple to get a warrant, then search Richard's home, and arrest him. However, in these times, criminals have a great many safeguards, and the word of a convicted felon such as Billy the Greek would be next to worthless in a trial court. The inspectors were faced with that well-known "moment of truth," when a decision had to be made whether to arrest Richards or to wait and develop more evidence.

After a conference of those working on the case and over the objections of some inspectors, it was decided to question non-criminal Richards. Inspectors visited him at his place of employment in Fall River, Massachusetts, where he admitted nothing. However, the inspectors came away with the opinion that he was lying. This gave him and his accomplices the knowledge that they were suspects and were being closed in on. Consequently they had a chance to move the loot if it was actually being held in Richards's home.

Inspectors immediately began watching Richards's home. He soon came out of the house and told them he might have something to say, after all. An inspector talked to Richards inside his home for a long time, and when he came out of the house, he said Richards had indicated that he was involved and that he was primarily concerned about how he might fare if he cooperated. The inspector related that Richards kept saying, "I won't have to go to jail, will I?"

Now that Richards had made some damaging statements, including an indication that he knew where the bulk of the money was hidden, the evidence was sufficient for the court to issue a search warrant. Richards's home was thoroughly searched, including the use of a backhoe to dig up his yard. No appreciable money was found, although a gun was turned up, which was sent to the identification laboratory. Neutron analysis determined that the clip from this gun had been used to drive nails that held cardboard on supports which were used to divert traffic at the roadblock at the time of the holdup, according to Inspector Raymond J. Dunne.

Inspector Raymond J. Dunne later interviewed Mrs. John J. Kelley, whose husband was reported to be the brains of the holdup. She voluntarily turned over some tape to him that was in the Kelley home after the holdup. When this tape was examined by the laboratory, it was found to be from the same roll that was used to bind the two postal drivers who were held up.

As the evidence mounted, Kelley and others retained F. Lee Bailey as their defense attorney. This was before any of them had been arrested or indicted. At the time the flamboyant Bailey also operated a private detective agency, and the inspectors soon found themselves subject to electronic eavesdropping. To complicate matters, it was reported that Billy the Greek then turned around and began giving the suspects information about the inspectors' investigations.

Among many who had to be interviewed was Robert Vincent Morency, who had been arrested in Nevada and returned to Seattle on a forgery warrant. This was in June 1965, almost three years after the Great Plymouth Mail Robbery. Morency told Seattle police officers that he knew a lot about the Plymouth robbery. Inspectors C. A. Hoyer and V. F. Worthington then talked to Morency several times.

The two men who were the gunmen in the holdup called each other Tony and Buster. Morency eventually told the inspectors that he was Tony. He actually did somewhat resemble the composite picture that had been sketched and distributed with the wanted circulars. Morency told several stories, but overall he showed a great deal of knowledge about the holdup, which could have been learned from reading press reports or from talking to other cons. After all, it had been three years since the holdup, and the Plymouth case was a well-known caper.

Morency said that Richards had brought him into the case. He named nine people as being involved, including John J. Kelley and a state trooper who worked out of the Bourne barracks on the Cape. He also said that the man called Buster was Buster Keaton, the other man in the composite picture exhibit.

Morency related how the gang had talked about taking this truck many times, but for a long time the police convoy was on. They had even devised plans to detour the troopers' cars away from the mail truck. When the trooper who was in on the plan told them that the convoy had been taken off, they decided to pull the job a few nights later.

Morency said that he wore a policeman's uniform on the night of the holdup. He said that he and Richards set up the roadblock at Reservation Road and that he approached the mail truck on the driver's side. At about the same time, Buster Keaton, also dressed in a policeman's uniform, reached the other side of the truck with a shotgun. After having the driver and guard lie down in the back of the truck, Morency then drove the truck four or five miles into the reservation.

After the holdup, Morency said, the nine-man gang met at Kelley's home, and all were surprised at the amount of money. Kelley said he didn't want any of the money left at his place, and Richards took most of the money, with Morency taking either three or four hundred thousand dollars. Morency said that he buried his share in a steel footlocker about ten feet deep in the backyard of his parents' home in New Bedford. He drew a diagram of the location and gave written authorization for an inspector or federal marshal to dig it up.

The Morency story was just one of the important leads that had to be followed up. It turned out that Morency had a record of mental trouble. His buried steel footlocker was never found by any law enforcement officer. It is doubtful that he in truth did participate in the holdup. In Seattle, Morency was trying to make a deal to clear up some criminal trouble he thought he was in back in New England. There was never any proof that his story was true.

By the summer of 1967 a great deal of hard evidence had been put together. Finally, the United States attorney in Boston had to either forget the case or move on it because the five-year statute of limitations was about to run out. Thomas R. Richards, John J. Kelley, and Mrs. Patricia Diaferio were named in an indictment with the holdup. Kelley and Mrs. Diaferio appeared for arraignment, but Richards has not been seen since that time. Without the testimony of Richards, much of the evidence could not be tied together. No one was ever convicted of the holdup.

This was to be a case where the boys in the black hats rode off into the night with the loot. The Post Office Department offered a reward of $50,000 leading to the arrest and conviction of those responsible, and the Federal Reserve reward for recovery of the currency was $150,000 or 10 percent of any part recovered. None of the rewards were ever claimed.

What did happen to the one and a half million in small bills? For one thing, there may not have been too much left. The services of criminal lawyers do not come cheap. There is the possibility that Richards made off with it, but the predominant belief is that he was "fitted with a cement overcoat" just before the trial.

14

Our Postal Problems

"NEITHER RAIN, NOR snow, nor gloom of night shall stay these couriers from the swift completion of their appointed rounds."

For over two centuries our postal service rumbled along happily performing a miracle of dependable and reliable service for those who entrusted their personal and business messages into its care.

Commerce could hardly have been carried on without the mail service, and untold days were made brighter when a letter from loved ones arrived. Anticipation of receiving mail is still looked forward to by a vast majority of the people.

But something has happened. People find it easier to telephone than to write, even those who are capable of writing. The corner mailbox where you formerly dropped your letters is either gone or is collected from so infrequently you must carry your mail to the nearest post office to feel halfway confident that it will get on its way.

You can no longer rely on local next-day delivery. If a holiday falls on a Monday, as most now do, you can't buy a money order or mail a parcel after 5:00 P.M. Friday until 8:00 A.M. the next Tuesday. If you live in a small town, mail is brought in once a day, no longer on Sundays or holidays.

Between 1968 and 1978, the cost of mailing a letter went from six cents to fifteen cents, a 150 percent increase, far ahead of inflation. On May 29, 1978, the cost of mailing a parcel went up 36.8 percent and third class 20 percent. The billion-dollar investment in bulk-mail-handling facilities that were operating below capacity before the 1978 postage raise may have to be sold to private parcel services at an extremely great loss. As late as November 15, 1951, you could mail a postal card for a penny; today it will cost ten cents.

Mail has been detained, delayed, stockpiled, and scheduled, usually in violation of law, to be worked at management's convenience, not the public's.

Postal reform has been tried over and over, but any noticeable improvement in overall service seems forever evasive.

Beginning as far back as 1953, a major reorganization was made as a result of the report of the Hoover Commission, which President Truman appointed to study the postal service. Among other recommendations, it was proposed that the postal service be decentralized. Before the adoption of the recommendations, most decisions had to be cleared through Washington, D. C.

When the Hoover Commission made its report, Jesse M. Donaldson was postmaster general. Donaldson was a man of exceptional ability and knew the postal service from the ground up. He had first worked in his father's post office at Hanson, Illinois, during summer vacations when he was going to school. Afterward, he was appointed as a letter carrier in Shelbyville, Illinois. In 1915 he received his appointment as postal inspector and was chief postal inspector from 1943 to 1945.

He said, "Decentralization will lead to the building of an immense political bureaucracy with little improvement in service." He declined to implement the Hoover Commission's recommendations. Time has clearly demonstrated that his judgment in this respect was exceptionally good.

After Dwight Eisenhower was elected president, Donaldson was succeeded by Republican Arthur Summerfield as postmaster general. Reorganization of the postal service was one of the first things the new postmaster general undertook, since improvement of the postal service had been a big campaign issue in 1952. On November 24, 1953, the first pilot regional office was established in Cincinnati. It administered most of Ohio, Indiana, and Kentucky.

Greater things were expected and promised. In announcing the establishment of the first regional office, Postmaster General Summerfield said it

1) would improve the service by permitting closer coordination allowing speedier solution of local problems;
2) would break the Washington bottleneck and that henceforth postmasters would report to their district managers;
3) would create efficiency and economy;
4) would improve employee morale by giving a more accessible ladder of advancement;
5) would permit regional management to make promotions, which would create a higher level of supervisory efficiency, since promotions will be made by those in a position to evaluate performance and capabilities accurately.

Staffs to man the new regional and district offices were to be selected almost exclusively from the ranks of career employees who had long experience in the postal service.

The reorganization was at least a major effort to do something. It is unfortunate it didn't work. The Postal Service is a gigantic complex organization that needs capable, experienced, and dedicated men with unusual ability to direct it. There were many such capable men in the service.

Samuel G. Schwartz, a postal inspector who had been in charge of the army postal service in the European theater during World War II was selected to help organize the pilot regional office in Cincinnati. During his military career he had demonstrated an ability as a talented organizer.

When the Cincinnati Region was successfully launched, others were formed, and Schwartz was named regional director of the Portland Region, which administered to the five states Alaska, Oregon, Washington, Idaho, and Montana.

In addition to being an excellent organizer, Director Schwartz was to demonstrate that he was also an effective empire builder. Starting early in 1954 in the old post office building in Portland, Oregon, with eight employees, his administrative staff prospered and grew like a cancer.

Schwartz did appoint and promote people from within the postal service, as promised by the postmaster general. It undoubtedly raised the hopes of many postal employees, if not their morale.

Director Schwartz made no secret of the fact that all appointments were subject to clearance by the Republican Central Committee. This did not entirely square with the postmaster general's promise of providing a more accessible ladder of advancement, because a Democrat had little chance to advance in the new bonanza.

Postal employees were prohibited from active political participation by the Hatch Act. As a consequence, even those known to have a political preference for the right party at the time often had difficulty obtaining political clearance.

The first regional engineer recommended by Director Schwartz was a postal inspector who had academic engineering training. He was a dedicated postal inspector, and it would have been unthinkable for him to have been involved actively in partisan politics. However, he had never made any secret of his political preferences. Nevertheless, the Republican Central Committee where he lived took some while to provide him with clearance. They had never had any reason to know what his political leanings might be.

The bureaucracy feared by Jesse Donaldson blossomed and grew fantastically. Soon there were fifteen regional offices. Administrative personnel steadily increased. Within three years regional administrative personnel rose from zero to 2,599.

The growth continues ever upward. As of June 20, 1975, there were 13,615 regional management employees, and the postal service is probably handling less mail. The number of workers, clerks, and letter carriers, on the other hand, has been reduced.

Regionalization accomplished the exact opposite of what was intended. The service did not improve, morale did not improve, paper passing increased, and rules and regulations that guide the postal service multiplied.

Summerfield was followed by Postmasters General J. Edward Day, John Gronouski, and Lawrence F. O'Brien. Each one earnestly tried to improve the service and operate an effective postal machine, but none of them were able to stay on the job long enough to accomplish much. No doubt each had many frustrations brought on by not having very much actual control over such a large organization.

Lawrence F. O'Brien, a very capable and tough organizer, had demonstrated his ability as a political strategist during the John F. Kennedy campaign. After the Kennedy years he was kept busy by President Lyndon B. Johnson, who appointed him Postmaster General on August 30, 1965.

He was called to Texas and sworn in at a very informal gathering in the small fourth-class post office at Hye, Texas. The post office occupies about twenty square feet of space in the back end of the Dieke Brothers Merchandise and Feed Store. It would normally be hard to find five people together all at one time anywhere in the vicinity of the Hye post office.

It is interesting to speculate what city-born-and-bred Larry O'Brien thought and felt during his induction as head of the largest business in the world as he stood with upraised hand in one of the smallest post offices he was to administer.

Why Hye, Texas? Hye served the summer White House, the L.B.J. Ranch, and a few local farmers nearby. If Larry O'Brien was surprised, so was Levi Dieke, the postmaster for thirty-four years. The president had given him no advance notice about the ceremony. He and his wife were away on vacation. He told me some premonition prompted him to return to Hye a day earlier than they had planned. It was then Levi Dieke learned that the following day the president would bring around a man to be sworn in as postmaster general.

The president was no stranger to Postmaster Dieke. They had been raised together, and Dieke could remember when he once shoved Lyndon in the Pedernales when they were boys. He said Lyndon usually had a reason for everything he did. By swearing O'Brien in as he did in the small Hye post office, he may have been trying to impress him with the fact that there were both very large and very small post offices serving the people.

Postmaster General O'Brien instituted a crash automation

program, expanded the office of planning and engineering, and attempted to correct some of the other problems. However, he was kept busy by the president, helping to push legislation through Congress. Thus his effectiveness with post office matters was diluted.

Just seventeen months after he was appointed he recommended doing away with his own job. He suggested that the post office should be free of congressional and executive control and should be made a public corporation, free to determine its costs, to set rates, to pay competitive wages, to develop work incentives, and to set up schools to train executives in modern techniques. O'Brien said he couldn't apply sound management practices because there was usually some antiquated law that prevented it.

It was time for another study, another reorganization, more postal reform. President Johnson did what President Truman had done years before. In 1968 he appointed a committee to make an exhaustive review of the structure and organization of the Post Office Department. Frederick R. Kappel was named chairman. After a profound study by well-qualified people, a report entitled "Toward Postal Excellence" was rendered.

This time the Post Office Department was to be separated from total government control. The postmaster general would no longer hold a cabinet post in the executive branch. The financial controls held by Congress would be lessened.

The National Association of Letter Carriers opposed the change. At the time, many considered the NALC to be the third strongest union in the United States. Affiliated with the AFL and CIO, the influence of the NALC on Congress was perfected to a fine degree. Many congressmen openly stated that without the support of the postal unions their chance of being elected would be slim.

When an issue was at stake, the NALC would bring letter carriers from almost every congressional district to Washington, hold a meeting, then have the carriers call on their respective congressmen and lobby for whatever pay raise or other legislation they wanted. They would buttonhole every congressman and ask how he was going to vote, then they would publish in their employee publications how each did vote. The procedure proved very effective. Few congressmen fought it; it was far more pleasant and practical to see their pictures in the employee magazines as friends of the postal employee.

Postage rates were to be set in the public interest based on actual cost of service. While the post office had various methods of determining costs, none of them were, or are, very accurate. It is generally agreed that first-class mail pays its own way. In 1968, studies showed that newspapers and magazines paid about 26 percent of the cost to deliver, while third-class circular mail came up with about 78 percent of the actual cost to deliver that class of mail.

The Kappel Commission's recommendations were never fully adopted. Compromises and adjustments had to be made with postal unions and organized mail users who fought many of the proposals.

Because the Kappel Report recommended each class of mail pay its own way, mailers of advertising matter fought the adoption. Newspaper and magazine publishers, who believed that their products were in the best national interest, felt that that class of mail should be partially subsidized for educational reasons, if for nothing more. Consequently, after compromise and piecemeal changes, a shattered Kappel Report was adopted. The U.S. Post Office Department became the U.S. Postal Service on July 1, 1971, and the postmaster general lost his seat in the president's cabinet.

The new Postal Service celebrated the change with a twenty thousand-dollar party paid for by the taxpayers. Postmaster General Winton Blount entertained the top brass in his reception room while the common workers were celebrating in the headquarters auditorium, according to a Washington, D.C., news report.

The spirit of the slogan "The mail must go through" was buried with the pony express emblem, which had been on the crests, badges, and letterheads. An eagle without wings, pointed in the opposite direction, became the new emblem, as if to predict the direction the new postal service was to take.

213

Amazingly, on February 3, 1971, P.M.G. Blount said that

1) More responsibility will be placed at local and regional levels;

2) There is no question that, once organized, the new system will speed the mail;

3) The organization will be run like a private business, rather than a red-tape-snarled government bureau; and

4) incentive will be restored by creating a chain of advancements and promotions from within, rather than filling posts by patronage.

If this sounded redundant to some, it is because Postmaster General Summerfield said about the same things seventeen years before, in 1953 when the Hoover Commission reforms were adopted. Postmaster General Blount also commented that the service was actually worse in 1971 than it was in 1953.

After telling America in 1971 what was to be done to provide a good postal service, now that it was a "corporation," Postmaster General Blount didn't stay around long enough to make good on his promise. He resigned in October 1972. Two years just isn't enough time to do a conscientious job as head of as large an organization as the U.S. Postal Service. When leaders fail to show interest and dedication, little can be expected down the ladder.

On March 29, 1973, the press announced that Blount Brothers Construction in Alabama had received the contracts to build large bulk-mail-handling centers in Detroit at twenty-two million dollars and in Des Moines at eighteen million dollars. The plants had been designed and sites chosen while Mr. Blount was postmaster general.

Nevertheless, when P.M.G. Blount took over the helm, things began to happen. His first step was to end the patronage system or at least to blunt its effectiveness. The regional-office structure had been functioning as political outposts and paper-passing machines. The career-development program was in a shambles. For example, in 1968 a level-five employee (about five thousand dollars a year) was promoted overnight to a top management position at level seventeen (about seventeen thousand dollars a year). That was like promoting a sergeant in the field to full colonel, but the man was vice-president of the postal clerks union, and it was politically smart to please employee unions. The fall before, a level-eight employee in the Anchorage post office was advanced to level thirteen. These are only two specific instances, but such unbelievable jumps did little to generate faith in a career-development program.

Blount had said that the postal unions were not really trade unions but were powerful lobbyists on Capitol Hill. Before he left, he was able to remove much of the partisan politics from the postal service. Naturally, some sort of politics had to fill this vacuum. For a long while it was obvious that if you had been employed by American or Continental Can, no matter how ineffective you may have been, your chance of obtaining a top postal position was strangely good. In-house career promotions became rare, except in the lower-paying positions.

Then the service cuts started. Blount was quoted as saying, "It seems kind of silly to me to have Saturday deliveries (of mail) to a business that is on a five-day week."

Early in 1973, no matter what it was called, the U.S. Postal Service was not taking care of the public's mail properly. Quietly and gradually, without publicity, cuts in service were continually being made. These cuts have never stopped. As late as July 1, 1977, the last railway post office was discontinued (New York to Washington, D.C.).

The new U.S. Postal Service didn't feel the older experienced supervisors could ever be trained to handle mail the way the new corporation wanted it handled. On May 12, 1971, a bonus of one half-year's pay was offered to those who were old enough to retire. With such enticement and pressure on the job mounting, many took retirement at a relatively young age. Instead of holding onto the competent, the U.S. Postal Service lost a wealth of nonreplaceable mail-moving experience by this costly move.

About January 6, 1973, two thousand sacks of Christmas mail were found at the Eugene, Oregon, post office, hidden out of sight. At the same time, 3,475 sacks were found in Charleston, West Virginia. This was a shocking example of how postal managers attempted to impress higher-ups with their efficiency in saving money. The new U.S. Postal Service had been given a free hand to improve the service, but delaying mail was not what was expected.

Having bled itself of the old hands, the U.S. Postal Service began filling exotic new positions, such as manager of creative services, computer technicians, social priorities specialists, psychologists, environmental officers, fringe benefit specialists, and lobby program officers. What such positions added to processing mail is a mystery.

Basically, mail is now handled on the sectional-center concept, which is tied in with the ZIP code. This means that a letter mailed in town A is hauled by postal vehicle to a mail-distribution center D, where it is distributed and then routed to town B. If town B happens to be only ten miles from town A, it is still hauled to center D, even if that entails a haul of over a hundred miles. Compared to the low cost of having mail transported directly to the point of address on scheduled trains and busses, this is a very costly and wasteful manner of moving mail.

A serious problem in working mail is the conglomerate of raw material that is mailed by the public in all sizes, shapes, and dimensions. Effective automation equipment could be built at a reasonable cost to sort standard-size pieces. Letters 6½ inches long and letters 9½ inches long of the same width could effectively be sorted by a simple machine. These two sizes readily accommodate about any letter the public would normally use. Any other size could be accepted but at a higher rate. Greeting-card manufacturers lobby against any attempt toward sensible standardization of letter mail.

For business purposes and government paperwork, a standard 9½-by-12-inch "flat" should be adequate. The ZIP code could then be typed or written in a small box preprinted on all envelopes. Then it would be economical to use accurate letter-scanning machines which would eliminate a vast amount of hand labor and would reduce the amount of missent mail and the cost of handling it.

How about parcels? At least a billion dollars is now tied up in bulk-mail-handling facilities, which are almost a disaster. The U.S. Postal Service continues to lose this business to private parcel

216

services. The bulk-mail-handling facility built in Phoenix, Arizona, in 1974 had to be closed after one month of operation. Cecil Goff, a member of the American Postal Workers, estimated the move to and from the facility cost fifty thousand dollars. The dock was too high for the trucks to back up to, there wasn't enough dock space to unload the mail, and the incoming and outgoing mail got mixed up. This building was "designed to provide space . . . for non-preferential mail-processing operations."

Few ever anticipated the mail service would be self-supporting. There are things the people do want at low cost in a postal service. One is newspapers and periodicals of literary or educational value. Another is low cost transportation of books.

It is in the public interest to have regular letter-mail service to every remote spot in the country. Whether or not individuals ever use such service, they are willing to pay to keep it going, should the need to use it ever arise. Furthermore, postal inspectors are devoted to keeping the mails secure, whereas private mail services do not have this capacity or experience. It is possible now to send mail to any remote point in the country. Most people will never need to send mail to Savoogna on St. Lawrence Island in the Bering Sea, but the service is there if you need it.

The U.S. Postal Service has lately initiated steps to promote the use of standard-size envelopes, whereas other countries have been doing this for years. Supposedly the USPS should be free to accomplish such things; but no, before anything can be done about regulating the size of letters or parcels, the slow Postal Rate Commission has to adopt such regulations.

The new USPS has improved productivity. When formed, it had 728,911 employees moving eighty-seven billion pieces of mail a year. By the middle of 1975, 702,000 employees moved eighty-nine billion pieces, and, despite warnings that small post offices would be closed, the number increased in ten years by 588.

Because of inability to do the work they are paid for, USPS management personnel are forced to contract for outside guidance. In 1975, Alnellum & Associates, along with other groups, were hired to determine the extent of delays to mail!

Post office facilities have been bought, leased, or rented as long as there has been a postal service. Certain space and equipment are needed to work the mail and service the necessary operations. For years what was called lease work of all phases was performed by only forty-five postal inspectors.

When the USPS "corporation" was first organized, it arranged with the U.S. Army Engineers to handle the space requirements and engineering needs. Army engineers were not acquainted with specific postal needs, and this arrangement was short-lived. Unable to do their own work, postal management then began to contract with appraisers and consultants to perform its space and requirement needs. The most effective of those who do this work are former postal employees who had experience in postal real estate or engineering before they retired.

Walter L. Robinson, a retired regional official of considerable high-level experience, has been doing appraisal and consulting work since his retirement years ago. When the U.S. Postal Service decided it should train its own men to do its own work, it contracted with Robinson to prepare a course of instruction in all phases of postal real estate and to write a textbook on the subject. The effort was pretty well wasted; the textbook was left unopened, so to speak.

When the training program was ready to go, the USPS found it was short of funds to implement the training of its own men, many of whom were already being paid to know the subject. The contracting goes on, a management cop-out.

Another blow to the staggering U.S. Postal Service is the Treasury Department's program to encourage retired people and others who receive regular government checks to have the checks deposited directly into their own bank accounts. This will save a vast amount of work.

It has been estimated that if all government checks issued on a regular recurring basis are electronically deposited into the recipients' bank accounts, the potential work loss to the USPS will be thirty-five billion checks a year. Recipients would simply have the amount of their monthly check automatically credited, and they will not need to wait for a bank deposit slip before they begin writing checks.

Obviously, taking millions of check letters out of the mail will save a great deal of work, eliminate theft, and consequently save money. It is surprising that it hasn't been done before. Every one of the thirty-five billion checks had to be made out, printed, placed in an envelope, separately mailed, and hand delivered every year!

Still another blow came from private enterprise. Convinced that the Postal Service was doomed to extinction, Thomas N. Murray of Oklahoma City launched his Independent Postal System of America, (IPSA) on February 15, 1968.

This alleged postal system was little more than an organized system for delivering advertising handbills and samples. It is unlawful for them to deliver first-class mail, and it is also unlawful to place anything other than U.S. Mail in house or rural mailboxes. By 1973, Murray's IPSA was operating in 454 cities in thirty-two states and claimed credit for delivering one hundred million pieces in fiscal year 1972.

Murray was reported to have started his IPSA with only five hundred dollars of his own money and fifty thousand dollars supplied by investors. Murray expanded IPSA through the sale of franchises of IPSA branches and routes. In a seventeen-month period after IPSA was founded, it claimed to have collected about two million dollars for routes in twenty-four cities.

This was not the first time there had been a private mail service in our country. The Constitutional Post Office was created in 1774 by William Goddard of Baltimore, Maryland. Goddard's postal service was also an instant success, and soon there were outlaw post offices in thirty-two communities. The reason for Goddard's success was attributed to one thing: in the interest of British national security, the king's postmen were opening mail of the colonists in an effort to identify subversives; Goddard's postmen appreciated the sanctity of the seal and protected the mail.

This first upstart mail service broke the British colonial postal service, but it was eliminated in 1798 by the new country when the mail service was taken over exclusively by the government.

IPSA and other private mail companies usually place their material in plastic bags that can be left attached to doorknobs or other handy places. The employees are dressed in uniforms sometimes quite similar to U.S. Postal Service letter carriers, and the average person usually doesn't notice the difference.

Noting Murray's success with IPSA, independent services sprang up throughout the country, many with considerable success. The American Postal Corporation claimed to have delivered more than one million pieces a year in heavily populated Orange County, Southern California. In Northern California, the National Postal Service claimed earnings of two million dollars a year for delivery of ninety-six million pieces. There were also the Hinsdale (Illinois) Common Carriers and the New England Carrier Service in Massachusetts. All in all, about a thousand independent mail services sprang up, offering delivery in heavily populated centers where their expenses would be low. Meanwhile, the U.S. Postal Service continued giving service to every small hamlet and to rural and isolated areas throughout the entire country.

After founding IPSA, Murray moved ahead boldly and rapidly. Prior to Christmas 1972, he decided it was time to move from handbill peddling to the delivery of real mail. He advertised in fifty-three cities that IPSA would deliver Christmas cards for five cents apiece, delivery being limited to certain ZIP code sections in heavily populated areas.

Since Christmas cards are personal messages, they are clearly classified as first-class mail. Murray no doubt knew he would be in violation of the Private Express Statutes, which gave the U.S. Postal Service a monopoly in the delivery of first-class mail. However, it was a good calculated risk. After all, insofar as anyone knew, the last time the monopoly called the Private Express Statutes had been tested was back in 1883 (U.S. v. Easson 18 F 590). Also, he may have been reassured because the old Post Office Department of cabinet rank had been reduced to a quasi-corporation called the U.S. Postal Service on July 1, 1971.

In cases like this, the postal inspectors have an obligation to investigate. And when there is a violation of federal law, the matter is presented to a United States attorney in the Department of

Justice for prosecution. Just what inspectors were doing in November and December of 1972 is not clear, but time was running short. James H. Rademacher, who was then president of the National Association of Letter Carriers, reported that his efforts to stir the Department of Justice into defending the laws of the United States was also without success. He had no more luck than the postal inspectors. Then Rademacher flew to Oklahoma City with his counsel and secured a temporary injunction against the IPSA plan to deliver Christmas cards.

A full hearing was set for December 10, at which time the Department of Justice finally entered the case as a friend of the court. Rademacher was questioned for two hours, and on December 15, the federal court issued a permanent injunction prohibiting anyone except the U.S. Postal Service from delivering letters, sealed or unsealed, with or without envelopes. The court commented that the monopoly rights of the U.S. Postal Service are unchallengeable and that the Constitution gave Congress the sole power to establish post offices and post roads. This monopoly had been upheld since the Republic was founded.

It was pointed out by Rademacher that if his Union had not taken the steps it did at the right time, the U.S. Postal Service either would have had to raise its rates in order to deliver what was left in the difficult and expensive areas or would have had to appeal for yet more subsidy from Congress.

Rademacher said, "This type of mail can easily be delivered by anyone at five cents apiece on a selective basis at a huge profit, leaving the isolated and difficult-to-serve areas without any mail service at all."

With the many varied and compounded pressures, the postal service can never be the same as it once was. Even in our affluent society, we cannot expect a service to meet the demands of an era that has grown accustomed to modern communication technology.

Our postal service was a grand tradition that can never fade as long as there are people who wish to keep their very personal messages sealed against the glaring lens of an inanimate automated machine and beyond the leering eyes of some machine operator.

As long as there are those who do not wish to whisper their secret love and intimate thoughts into a telecommunication system where someone could eavesdrop, there will be a postal service. As long as there is a need to retain some written record of an agreement, a contract or a pledge, there will be a postal service. As long as people are free to read the printed word and are rejuvenated when a letter from some loved one arrives, there will be a postal service.

Only as long as our nation is free will there be a postal service.

Index